The Changing Family

ISSUES

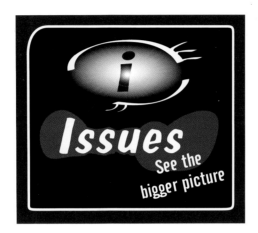

Volume 191

Series Editor

Lisa Firth

Educational Publishers
Cambridge

First published by Independence
The Studio, High Green
Great Shelford
Cambridge CB22 5EG
England

© Independence 2010

Photocopy licence

The material in this book is protected by copyright. However, the
purchaser is free to make multiple copies of particular articles for instructional
purposes for immediate use within the purchasing institution.
Making copies of the entire book is not permitted.

British Library Cataloguing in Publication Data

The changing family. -- (Issues ; v. 191)

1. Parenting. 2. Families.

I. Series II. Firth, Lisa.

306.8'74-dc22

ISBN-13: 978 1 86168 542 1

Printed in Great Britain

MWL Print Group Ltd

CONTENTS

Chapter 1 Family Trends

Chapter 2 Working Parents

OTHER TITLES IN THE ISSUES SERIES

For more on these titles, visit: www.independence.co.uk

EXPLORING THE ISSUES
Photocopiable study guides to accompany the above publications. Each four-page A4 guide provides a variety of discussion points and other activities to suit a wide range of ability levels and interests.

A note on critical evaluation

Because the information reprinted here is from a number of different sources, readers should bear in mind the origin of the text and whether the source is likely to have a particular bias when presenting information (just as they would if undertaking their own research). It is hoped that, as you read about the many aspects of the issues explored in this book, you will critically evaluate the information presented. It is important that you decide whether you are being presented with facts or opinions. Does the writer give a biased or an unbiased report? If an opinion is being expressed, do you agree with the writer?

The Changing Family offers a useful starting point for those who need convenient access to information about the many issues involved. However, it is only a starting point. Following each article is a URL to the relevant organisation's website, which you may wish to visit for further information.

Marriage, relationships and family trends

Information from the Family and Parenting Institute.

P arents' relationship with each other affects their children's wellbeing. Does the state have any power to influence this and should it?

Key statistics:

⇨ In 2006, there were 236,980 weddings in England and Wales, of which 39 per cent were remarriages for one or both parties.[1]

⇨ There were 132,562 divorces in England and Wales in 2006, the lowest divorce rate since 1984.[2]

⇨ While marriage rates have fallen steadily since the early 1970s when there were over 450,000 a year, divorce rates have remained relatively constant over the same period.[3]

⇨ In 1971, the mean age of men and women at first marriage was 24 and 22, respectively. By 2004, it was 31 for men and 29 for women.[4]

⇨ In 2006, 23 per cent of children in Great Britain were

living in lone parent families. This has increased from 21 per cent in 1997 and seven per cent in 1972.[5]

⇨ 37 per cent of children of lone parents live in poverty in the UK (under than 60 per cent of median household income before housing costs) compared to 18 per cent of children in couple families.[6]

⇨ In 2006, 56 per cent of births in the UK were to married couples.[7] The majority of the remainder were to cohabiting parents (estimated three-fifths in England and Wales, 2005).[8]

More support is needed for couples to build strong, resilient relationships, including support for parents and children during and after relationship breakdown.

⇨ Divorce and separation can increase the chances of poor outcomes for children. However, these are not inevitable. The likelihood of poor outcomes is increased by financial hardship; family conflict before, during and after separation; and multiple changes in family structure. Quality contact with the non-resident parent can improve outcomes.[9]

> **It is not just parental separation that has an impact on children: the quality of their parents' relationship also affects their wellbeing**

⇨ It is not just parental separation that has an impact on children: the quality of their parents' relationship also affects their wellbeing. In research commissioned by FPI, seven out of ten young people, in contrast to only a third of adults, said that it was important that parents should get on well together in order to raise happy children.[10]

⇨ Both prevention and crisis intervention are needed, starting in schools with a focus on relationships as well as biological sex education. Relationship support and advice should be easily available from magazines, helplines, health visitors, schools and family workers. Support for parents and children

FAMILY AND PARENTING INSTITUTE

before, during and after separation needs to be dramatically improved, with a focus on child-inclusive mediation.

Financial incentives for married couples would be counterproductive

⇨ Benefits to married couples at the expense of others are a risky strategy. In the short term they will penalise children who are already worse off, in the hope of influencing behaviour to create more stable relationships in the long term. This is doubtful because:

↳ The financial incentive would be small compared to the difference between maintaining a household with one adult or with two.

↳ Even supposing that they did encourage cohabiting couples to marry for financial reasons, it is not known to what extent the marriage bond creates relationship stability as opposed to more stable couples choosing to marry.

The debate needs to be shifted from moral panic about a decline of the nuclear family and a rise in single parents, towards evidence-based policy

⇨ Sweden, Denmark and Norway, ranked highest in the 2007 UNICEF report on child wellbeing, have similar proportions of children in lone-parent families to the UK, but a much lower child poverty rate.[11] These countries are notable for their high-quality childcare and are much more equal societies than the UK.

⇨ In 2005, more than ten per cent of all families with dependent children in Great Britain were stepfamilies.[12]

⇨ These families face particular challenges which should be recognised in Government policy.

Claire James, Family and Parenting Institute

Notes

1 Office for National Statistics (2008) Marriages: 4% fall in UK marriages. Online at: http://www.statistics.gov.uk/cci/nugget.asp?id=322

2 Office for National Statistics (2008) Divorces: Divorces fall by 7% in 2006. Online at: http://www.statistics.gov.uk/cci/nugget.asp?id=170

3 Office for National Statistics (2007) *Social Trends*. Palgrave Macmillan

4 Office for National Statistics (2008) *Social Trends*. Palgrave Macmillan

5 Office for National Statistics (2007) *Social Trends*. Palgrave Macmillan

6 Department for Work and Pensions (2008) Households Below Average Income (HBAI) 1994/95-2006/07. Department for Work and Pensions

7 Office for National Statistics (2008) *Social Trends*. Palgrave Macmillan

8 Office for National Statistics (2007) *Social Trends*. Palgrave Macmillan

9 Rodgers, B. and Pryor, J. (1998) *Divorce and separation: the outcomes for children*. Joseph Rowntree Foundation

In 2006 there were 236,980 weddings in England and Wales, of which 39 per cent were remarriages for one or both parties

10 National Family and Parenting Institute (2000) Teenagers' attitudes to parenting: A survey of young people's experiences of being parented, and their views on how to bring up children. Survey conducted by MORI

11 UNICEF (2007) Child Poverty in Perspective: An Overview of Child Well-being in Rich Countries. Innocenti Report Card 7. Unicef

12 Office for National Statistics (2007) *Social Trends*. Palgrave Macmillan

Updated June 2008

⇨ The above information is reprinted with kind permission from the Family and Parenting Institute. Visit www.familyandparenting.org for more information.

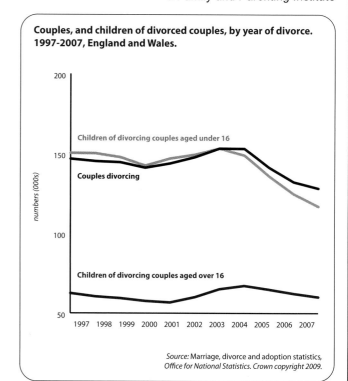

Couples, and children of divorced couples, by year of divorce. 1997-2007, England and Wales.

Source: Marriage, divorce and adoption statistics, Office for National Statistics. Crown copyright 2009.

FAMILY AND PARENTING INSTITUTE

Data shows continuing changes to marriage and society in the UK

Information from Ekklesia.

By 2031, three out of five adults in Britain may be unmarried, say forecasters extrapolating from data compiled by the Office for National Statistics (ONS). The shift reflects significant changes in social and family structure.

Married couples could make up 41 per cent of the over-16 population in 20 years time. The figure is 49 per cent now. Single people, divorcees, lone parents and cohabiting couples will outnumber them.

But the majority of people will still be in committed relationships of one kind or another. Cohabiters are projected to rise from 4.5 million to 7.4 million.

However, it is predicted that the fastest-growing group will be those who remain single.

There are at present some 21.7 million married people in England and Wales, compared with 14.9 million adults who have never married

Some commentators are suggesting that the decline in legally sanctioned marriage that began some decades ago will reduce it to the status of 'a minority lifestyle' but others say this is an alarmist and selective interpretation.

There are at present some 21.7 million married people in England and Wales, compared with 14.9 million adults who have never married. Four million people are divorcees and three million are widowed.

The ONS states: 'There were 270,000 weddings in the UK in 2007, a fall of 2.7 per cent since 2006. Marriages registered in England and Wales fell by 3.3 per cent in 2007 to 231,450, which is the lowest number of marriages since 1895 (228,204). In Scotland, marriages decreased slightly from 29,898 in 2006 to 29,866 in 2007, while in Northern Ireland marriages increased five per cent to 8,687. The long-term picture for UK weddings is one of decline from a peak of 480,285 marriages in 1972.

'In England and Wales, the number of unmarried adults rose in 2007, but the number who chose to marry fell, producing the lowest rates since marriages were first calculated in 1862. In 2007, the marriage rate for men was 21.6 men marrying per 1,000 unmarried men aged 16 and over, down from 23.0 in 2006. The marriage rate for women in 2007 was 19.7 women marrying per 1,000 unmarried women aged 16 and over, down from 20.7 in 2006.

'The number of marriages in England and Wales that were the first for both partners peaked in 1940 at 426,100 when 91 per cent of all marriages were the first for both partners. This number has since fallen to 143,440 in 2007, accounting for 62 per cent of all marriages.

'Remarriages rose by about a third between 1971 and 1972, following the introduction of the Divorce Reform Act 1969 in England and Wales and then levelled off. In 2007, 88,010 marriages were remarriages for one or both parties, accounting for 38 per cent of all marriages.

'Since 1992 there have been more civil ceremonies in England and Wales than religious ceremonies. In 2007, civil ceremonies accounted for 67 per cent of all ceremonies which is an increase from 61 per cent in 1997.'

In a little over 20 years there could be 22.1 million people who have never married – 42 per cent of the adult population – against 21.6 million husbands and wives.

2031 Old customs and traditions #29
MARRIAGE

Picture above: this couple bravely keeps alive this antiquated institution.

Anastasia de Waal, author of *Second Thoughts on the Family*, published in May 2008, commented: 'Many more are living at home with their parents, which is a bit of a killer for romance. Others are living far from their work and find it difficult to meet people.'

Her book acknowledged the trends confirmed by the latest Office of National Statistics data, but she argued that marriage was 'not so much out of fashion but out of reach' for those feeling the economic pinch and not in secure employment.

Researchers also point out that while people are living in a greater diversity of family, kinship and friendship-based relationships these days, the decision to commit permanently, though receding, is still the goal that a majority of people aspire to.

Lesbian and gay people are also arguing that their partnerships should be given the full status of marriage as in South Africa, some parts of the USA and six European nations, including Sweden from May 2009.

In a little over 20 years there could be 22.1 million people who have never married – 42 per cent of the adult population – against 21.6 million husbands and wives

Simon Barrow, co-director of the religion and society think-tank Ekklesia, said that it was important not to rush to 'alarmist' conclusions about the latest ONS data, but rather to invest in supporting relationships, to recognise extended and informal families as well as nuclear ones and to re-visit the nature of marriage in the light of changing social and religious patterns.

'The vast majority of people – whether religious or otherwise – recognise that stable, faithful, loving, just and lasting relationships are crucial for the health of society and the nurturing of children,' he said. 'We need to build on that and offer practical support and example. Official agencies, community organisations, charities, faith groups, schools and families all have a role to play.

'The key issue is to look at how people can be helped to respond to the intense pressures they are under in modern life – from economic insecurity and consumerism right through to false expectations about romance and desire disconnected from the tough work of commitment.

'It is important not to be seduced by simple headlines about marriage and family. These days, more people are committing to relationships because they want to, not because they are coerced. Equality between the sexes is rightly encouraged. Abusive relationships are being challenged. Civil partnerships are being entered into. We need to look at what is healthy as well as harmful in the changes we see taking place,' said Barrow.

Campaigners say that addressing unemployment, economic inequality, poor education, social alienation and child poverty are vital to supporting families. People who are poor and without regular income are more likely to be unmarried or separated.

It is predicted that the fastest-growing group will be those who remain single

In 2006, Ekklesia called for a radical reconsideration of the meaning of marriage, both on the part of the state and general society and in faith communities. It says that the ONS-reported growth of civil ceremonies and the decline in religious ones, as well as the social challenges to the inherited family structures reinforce this need.

In its *What Future for Marriage?* report, the think-tank said that the legal-contractual function of the civic authorities and the spiritual role of blessing and supporting relationships in the church are too easily confused and argued that consideration should be given to a variety of recognised civil partnerships through which couples could specify the type of legal commitment they wished to make to one another – with the churches and others being free to decide how to respond to them.

This is similar to the kind of pattern adopted in other parts of Europe, including those where gay marriage has been legally recognised.

The report said: 'This would allow both civic and religious authorities autonomy in decision-making, would avoid people having to make vows they do not believe in [,] and would encourage couples to think more seriously about the kind of commitment they wanted to enter into, and the consequences of this for others.'

See: Ekklesia, What Future for Marriage? – *http://tinyurl. com/dydqee*
Office of National Statistics on marriage in the UK, 1951–2007 – http://www.statistics.gov.uk/cci/nugget. asp?id=322
3 April 2009

⇨ The above information is reprinted with kind permission from Ekklesia. Visit www.ekklesia.co.uk for more information.

© Ekklesia

EKKLESIA

What's your parenting style?

Do you run your family like an army general? Or are you so relaxed that teatime's more like a chimp's tea party? Read this article to find out what your 'parenting style' is. By Dr Clare Bailey at Parenting Matters, www.parentingmatters.co.uk

Have you ever wondered whether you're much stricter than other parents? Or perhaps if you're more laid back than most? Or even too indulgent with your children? Many parents watch how other parents respond to their children and wonder whether they would have reacted in the same way in that situation.

I was in great admiration of a mother with a very chatty and enthusiastic three-year-old in the supermarket recently, she was talking through the items on her shopping list and encouraging her son to find them and put them in the trolley – I would have struggled with the temptation to race round quickly and get the job done. And then you see the familiar scenario of a parent giving in to the wails for sweets at the checkout. Is the first parent more child-centred and the other more permissive? Most parents have a sense of what sort of parent they are, be it strict, laid back or somewhere in between, yet it can be interesting to see how our 'parenting styles' compare with others and to get a clearer idea of what sort of parent we really are.

All parents have their own unique blend of 'parenting styles', which simply means we have a preferred pattern of responses when with our children. For example, we all lie on a spectrum between 'being engaged' and 'being uninvolved' or between 'being strict' and 'being relaxed'. Although this will vary according to the age and personality of the child, we each have a particular approach which tends to become the 'automatic' or 'default' style, especially when under pressure. The approach you fall back on is often determined by how you were brought up, your own personality, culture or simply what you have picked up from those around you.

Research shows that there are four main parenting styles (D. Baumrind, Maccoby & Martin); do you recognise yourself?

1 Balanced-authoritative. This is in some ways the ideal parenting style, balancing clear limits and appropriate expectations with warmth and involvement (as with the mum involving her son with shopping and making it fun). However, she would probably not allow him to add a bumper bag of Mars bars to the trolley, and would explain why.

2 Permissive-indulgent. These parents are warm and engaged with their children but with fewer or inconsistent limits and expectations. They would be more inclined to give in at the checkout as they hate to see their child upset, despite explaining how sweets will rot teeth.

3 Hands-off. These parents tend to be laissez-faire, less involved and with fewer boundaries. They probably won't notice the additions to the trolley or mind very much anyway.

4 Authoritarian-strict. Here there's a stronger emphasis on control and clear limits above warmth and involvement. They may not let their child out of the trolley and would stick firmly to what's on the list.

These different styles have been found to have an impact on how children respond and develop. Although most parents have a natural or automatic parenting style, this isn't set in stone.

> *All parents have their own unique blend of 'parenting styles', which simply means we have a preferred pattern of responses when with our children*

Understanding our 'automatic' tendencies may be the first step towards change. By developing and fine-tuning their parenting skills, parents often find they naturally move towards a more balanced approach. This can reduce conflict, help improve your relationship with your child and produce happier, more confident and capable children.

If you'd like to find out more about your parenting style, check out the online quiz at www.parentingmatters. co.uk. Based on extensive research, this quiz will give you detailed feedback on your type of parenting style and what it means for you and your family.

24 November 2009

⇨ The above information appears on the Families Chiltern website and is reprinted with kind permission from Dr Claire Bailey. Visit www.familiesonline.co.uk for more.

© Dr Clare Bailey

FAMILIES CHILTERN

'Character' is the key to social mobility

'Tough love' parents who combine warmth and discipline are better at building good character capabilities in their children, finds a major new report from the think tank Demos.

Character capabilities – application, self-regulation and empathy – make a vital contribution to life chances, mobility and opportunity. For those who turned 30 in 1988, character capabilities barely impacted on their economic success. But in just over a decade, these skills became central to life chances: for those who turned 30 in 2000, character capabilities had become 33 times more important in determining earnings.

The development of these character capabilities is profoundly shaped by the experience of a child in the pre-school years. Children with 'tough love' parents were twice as likely to develop good character capabilities by age five as children with 'disengaged' parents, and did significantly better than children with 'laissez faire' or 'authoritarian' parents. The *Building Character* report, which analysed longitudinal data from over 9,000 households in the UK, found that eight per cent of families have parents that are 'disengaged', which is approximately 600,000 families.

Children with married parents, both of whom are a biological parent, are twice as likely to develop good character capabilities than children from lone-parent or step-parented families

Parental confidence is also vital to developing character capabilities. Children of parents who rank themselves poorly in terms of their own parenting ability are less likely to develop key character skills.

Building Character looked at the effect the following factors had on infant character development:

Income

⇨ Children from the richest income quintile are more than twice as likely to develop strong character capabilities than children from the poorest quintile.

⇨ Children from the poorest income quintile are three times less likely to develop strong character capabilities than children from the richest quintile.

⇨ While 'tough love' parenting is less frequent in low-income backgrounds, the 'love' element was consistently distributed throughout economic groups. Consistent rule-setting and authoritative parenting was associated with wealthier families, indicating a need for parents to set more consistent discipline and boundaries in lower income groups.

Children with cohabiting parents fare slightly worse than those with married parents, but better than those with lone parents or step-parents

⇨ When parental style and confidence are factored in, the difference in child character development between richer and poorer families disappears, showing that parenting is the most important factor influencing character development.

Family structure

⇨ Children with married parents, both of whom are a biological parent, are twice as likely to develop good character capabilities than children from lone-parent or step-parented families.

⇨ Children with cohabiting parents fare slightly worse than those with married parents, but better than those with lone parents or step-parents.

⇨ When parental style and confidence is factored in, the relationship between family structure and child character development disappears almost entirely, showing that parenting is the most important factor influencing character development.

Other factors

⇨ The primary carer's level of education has a positive effect on developing character capabilities.

⇨ Breast-feeding to six months has a positive effect on developing character capabilities.

⇨ Girls are more likely to develop character capabilities by the age of five.

DEMOS

⇨ There is no connection between paid employment on behalf of either parent and the development of character capabilities.

The report found that while there are links between income and family structure, and the development of character, parental ability significantly diminishes these factors, making parental style and confidence the most important tools in improving social mobility.

'The foundations for our character are laid before the age of five. This puts a huge emphasis on parenting, but...it is confidence, warmth and consistent discipline that matter most'

Based on the research conducted for this report, the goals for policy should be to:

⇨ Strengthen provision of support and information to parents to help them incubate character capabilities in their children.

⇨ Focus support on disadvantaged children – those with 'disengaged' parents and those from low income groups – which have greater susceptibility to the quality of their care and poorly performing parents.

⇨ Ensure quality control and value for money in early years' intervention.

An ambitious agenda for equality of opportunity will need to take the development of character capabilities seriously. *Building Character* includes the following policy recommendations:

⇨ Refocus Sure Start as a tool for early intervention: Sure Start should be less focused on childcare and more focused on child development, particularly parent-child interaction. Sure Start could also act as a more effective hub for creating peer relationships and local networks that can be central to parental support.

⇨ Improve pilots for the Family Nurse Partnership: while a promising model to follow from the US, before the pilots are rolled out nationally, there must be more evidence for how an FNP should work in a UK context.

⇨ Give health visitors an early years' role: more emphasis should be placed on health visitors' role in identifying and supporting positive parenting. Health visitors should carry out a 'Half-Birthday Check-up' to monitor progress and identify families that need extra support.

⇨ Set up a 'NICE' for evidence-based parenting interventions: a national body to 'kitemark' successful, evidence-based parenting programmes would aid local commissioners to invest in programmes that are proven to work.

Jen Lexmond, principal author of the report, said:

'Character, something we tend to think of as a "soft skill", has the most profound effect on a person's life. Far from a "soft" skill, character is integral to our future success and wellbeing.

'The foundations for our character are laid before the age of five. This puts a huge emphasis on parenting, but whatever the parental background, it is confidence, warmth and consistent discipline that matter most.'

8 November 2009

⇨ The above information is reprinted with kind permission from Demos. Visit www.demos.co.uk for more information.

© *Demos*

DEMOS

Divorces in England and Wales

Information from the Office for National Statistics

The number of divorces in England and Wales fell by 5.0 per cent in 2008 to 121,779 compared with 128,232 in 2007. This is the fifth consecutive year that the number of divorces has fallen, from a peak of 153,176 in 2003, and is the lowest number since 1975 when there were 120,522 divorces. The number of divorces was highest amongst men and women aged 40 to 44.

In 2008, the divorce rate in England and Wales decreased by 5.1 per cent to 11.2 divorcing people per 1,000 married population, compared with 11.8 in 2007. The 2008 divorce rate is the lowest since 1979, when there were also 11.2 divorces per 1,000 married people.

Compared with 2007, divorce rates in England and Wales for both men and women fell across many age groups. However, rates increased for men aged under 20 and over 60 and for women aged 50 to 59.

Half of couples divorcing in 2008 had at least one child aged under 16

For the fourth consecutive year, both men and women in their late twenties had the highest divorce rates of all five-year age groups. In 2008, there were 22.8 divorces per 1,000 married men aged 25 to 29 and 26.0 divorces per 1,000 married women aged 25 to 29. This compared with 16.5 divorces per 1,000 married men aged 45 to 49 and 14.5 divorces per 1,000 married women aged 45 to 49 in 2008.

The mean age at divorce increased for both men and women in 2008. The mean age for men divorcing was 43.9 years in 2008, an increase from 43.7 years in 2007. For women this increased from 41.2 years in 2007 to 41.4 years in 2008. Since 1998, the mean age at divorce for both men and women has increased by 3.5 years from 40.4 years for men and 37.9 years for women.

The median duration of marriage at divorce granted in 2008 was 11.5 years, a decrease from 11.7 years in 2007 and an increase from 10.2 years in 1998.

In 2008, 20 per cent of men divorcing and 20 per cent of women divorcing had a previous marriage ending in divorce. These proportions have almost doubled since 1981 when they were 11 per cent. Out of all divorces in 2008, 69 per cent were to couples where the marriage was the first for both parties while the remaining 31 per cent were to couples where at least one of the party had been previously divorced or widowed.

In 2008, of all decrees awarded to one partner (rather than jointly to both), 67 per cent were awarded to the wife. In over half of the cases where the divorce was granted to the wife, the husband's behaviour was the fact proven. Of the divorces granted to the husband, the most common facts proven were the wife's behaviour (34 per cent of cases) and two years' separation with consent (32 per cent of cases).

Half of couples divorcing in 2008 had at least one child aged under 16. There were 106,763 children aged under 16 who were in families where the parents divorced in 2008, a decrease of 29 per cent from 1998 when there were 150,129 children. Over one-fifth (21 per cent) of the children in 2008 were under five and 63 per cent were under 11. In 2008, there was an average of 1.76 children under 16 per divorcing couple (that had children aged under 16).

The number of divorces in the United Kingdom fell by 5.5 per cent in 2008 to 136,026 compared with 143,955 in 2007.

The number of divorces in Scotland fell by 10 per cent from 12,810 in 2007 to 11,474 in 2008. The number of divorces in Northern Ireland also decreased. In 2008, there were 2,773 divorces, 4.8 per cent less than in 2007 when there were 2,913.

28 January 2010

⇨ The above information is reprinted with kind permission from the Office for National Statistics. Visit www.statistics.gov.uk for more information.

© Crown copyright

Impact of family breakdown on children's wellbeing

Evidence review by Ann Mooney, Chris Oliver and Marjorie Smith, Thomas Coram Research Unit, Institute of Education, University of London.

Parental separation and its impact on children is a key issue in public policy. Although wanting to support stable parental relationships, the Government also wants to provide the necessary support to optimise positive outcomes for children where parental relationships do break down. This review of the impact of parental separation and divorce on children's wellbeing and development was undertaken to inform policy development. It incorporates evidence concerning family breakdown and its consequences, and includes research relating to both married and cohabiting parents.

Key findings

⇨ Family breakdown is not a discrete event, but a process that involves a number of risk and protective factors that interact in complex ways both before and after parental separation.

⇨ Although children are at increased risk of adverse outcomes following family breakdown, and negative outcomes can persist into adulthood, the difference between children from intact and non-intact families is small and the majority of children will not be adversely affected in the long term.

⇨ Children from both intact and non-intact families vary widely in their experiences. Family functioning appears to have greater impact on outcomes for children than does family type, with outcomes for many children experiencing family breakdown as good as, or even better than, those for children from intact families.

⇨ Evidence indicates that there is no direct causal relationship between family breakdown and negative child outcomes. Instead, a number of factors such as parental conflict, the quality of parenting and of parent-child relationships, maternal mental health and financial hardship, interact in complex ways to increase or limit the risk of adverse outcomes following family breakdown.

⇨ Conflict and stress can affect the ability of parents, whether together, separated or divorced, to parent effectively, which in turn impacts on children's wellbeing.

⇨ Poverty and the stress it brings is both a contributor to family breakdown and frequently a consequence of it. Children from poorer backgrounds, whether from intact or non-intact families, generally do less well on a number of measures compared with children from more advantaged backgrounds.

⇨ Parental separation and divorce can lead to repeated changes in family structure. These transitions often involve other changes, such as moving house, school or neighbourhood, and the loss of contact with the extended family. Such multiple transitions and consequent changes increase the risk of negative child outcomes.

⇨ Children's positive adjustment to family breakdown is associated with a number of factors. These include competent and warm parenting, parents having good mental health, low parental conflict, cooperative parenting post separation, and social support. Children also benefit from contact with the non-resident parent (usually the father), but not when this relationship is poor or contact is against the child's wishes.

June 2009

⇨ The above information is reprinted with kind permission from the Department for Communities and Local Government. Please visit www.dclg.gov.uk for more information.

DEPARTMENT FOR COMMUNITIES AND LOCAL GOVERNMENT

A new family

The fun and hard work of building a stepfamily.

By Christine Tufnell

Stepfamilies are the fastest growing family type in the UK. Over one-third of us are part of the stepfamily experience.

Your grandchildren may be about to have a new step-parent, or your son/daughter may be married to someone who already has children. Perhaps you have children from a first marriage and you're now marrying again, or you have become dad or mum to someone else's children.

So what is it like to build a stepfamily?

Sally and Keith have been married and building their stepfamily for just ten months. They say they never realised how difficult it was going to be, and how dramatic the changes would be.

'We just focused on the wedding and all the other stuff was overlooked,' Keith admits. 'As we had both been married before it was assumed we knew all about it!'

'We were asked just two weeks before the wedding if we had forgiven our ex-partners. We said yes, but wondered what would have happened if we had said no! We did discuss a lot of things together, and have now talked to an older couple, and attended a day conference.'

Balancing being a wife and a mother

Sally adds: 'I didn't find my first marriage difficult, so I suppose I was a bit naïve and thought I wouldn't find number two difficult.

'When I was married before, we were DINKYs – Double Income No Kids. My son Joshua was born after my husband left, so when I was a mother, I wasn't a wife any more. I had five years as a working single parent. And then suddenly, I was a wife again, and a stepmother to two teenage daughters, while still working full time and being the biological mother to my son.

'I had never had the experience of having to balance being a wife and a mother. I didn't have to worry if my husband was getting upset or not getting attention. My whole focus was on my child. That's what we struggle with now. I don't give Keith that time which he rightly thinks he ought to have, because I am looking after Joshua.'

The challenge for Sally has also been taking on teenagers (14 and 19) who are not related to her. 'They have mood swings and are very different from me,' she says. 'But

they gave me cards for Mothering Sunday, and Amy gave me a card when I was unwell saying they would look after me. I really appreciated that.'

Keith feels that no matter how hard you work at it, there will always be a sense of 'my daughters, your son'.

'I have an unconditional love for my daughters which is more forgiving,' he says. 'But I do want to be a father figure to Joshua. It makes a difference that he is quite young. When we first married, if we were in the kitchen and I gave Sally a cuddle, Joshua would try to separate us. Now he joins in for a three-way hug.'

A new name

'Joshua has always called me Keith. We have great fun times together, but at other times he doesn't want me near him and I can feel rejected.

'But then recently he and I were in the supermarket, getting food for lunch. We were chatting away and, when we reached the cake aisle, Joshua announced, "I'm not going to call you Keith any more. I have a new name for you." I was wondering what he was going to call me now – he has said I'm lazybones for lying in bed! He said, "I'm going to call you Dad." And he has kept this up ever since. It's really encouraging. You have to be patient.'

The girls are pleased that their dad is married, as they want him to be happy, but it isn't always easy for them. Everyone enjoyed last Christmas together, but at the end Amy said, 'It was a great day but I wished we could have Mum and Dad like we used to.'

But as Keith says, the new family has not yet built up shared memories. They are on their first family holiday this summer, which should be creating some memories for them.

'I believe it will be a very different picture in four or five years,' Keith concludes. 'We're still working through the baggage – ours and the children's. Talking with others has helped us to see all the positives and not to focus so much on the negatives.'

Stepfamilies – are they a challenge? Yes. Are they hard work? Yes. Are they fun? Yes. Are they worthwhile? Yes. Can they last? Yes – my stepson of 21 years has recently written to me: 'If Dad dies before you, we will always be there for you. You can count on our love and support for the rest of your life.'

⇨ The above information is reprinted with kind permission from Care for the Family. Visit www.careforthefamily.org.uk for more information.

CARE FOR THE FAMILY

Broken families and paternal contact

Third of family break-up children lose contact with fathers in 'failing' court system, says poll.

Tens of thousands of children a year are losing contact with their fathers because of a 'failing' family court system and disastrous custody arrangements, a study has found.

One in three children whose parents separated or divorced over the last 20 years disclosed that they had lost contact permanently with their father.

Almost a tenth of children from broken families said the acrimonious process had left them feeling suicidal while others later sought solace in drink, drugs or crime.

They complained of feeling 'isolated' and 'used' while parents admitted having used children as 'bargaining tools' against each other.

Lawyers said the study showed that the court system itself was making family break-up more acrimonious with children used as 'pawns'.

One in three children whose parents separated or divorced over the last 20 years disclosed that they had lost contact permanently with their father

They warned that so-called 'no fault' divorces were encouraging warring parents to channel their 'bloodletting' into disputes over contact.

Opposition politicians said the poll presented an alarming picture of a system 'in a mess' which was all too often leaving fathers 'shut out'.

The poll of 4,000 parents and children was carried out to provide a snapshot of the workings of the family court system exactly 20 years after the implementation of the landmark 1989 Children Act.

It found that a third of children from broken families had been tempted by drink or drugs while as many as ten per cent had later become involved in crime.

A quarter of the children said that they had been asked to lie to one parent by the other and 15 per cent said they had even been called on to 'spy' for their mother or father.

Meanwhile half of parents polled admitted deliberately drawing out the legal process for maximum benefit and more than two thirds conceded that they had used their children as 'bargaining tools'.

About 250,000 couples, both married and non-married, separate every year affecting 350,000 kids, according to the Department for Children, Schools and Families.

'The adversarial nature of the system invites people to come and use the courts system as a punch up and the children get used as pawns,' said Sandra Davis, head of family law at Mishcon de Reya, for whom the poll was conducted.

'It polarises parents and it puts children in the middle of the antagonism.

'Some fathers back off because it is too painful to carry on litigating, they give up.'

Tim Loughton, the Tory Shadow children's minister, said: 'This is alarming evidence of the very detrimental impact it is having on the welfare of the children themselves.'

'Clearly, the court system is failing and is positively encouraging conflict – and continuing conflict.'

Iain Duncan Smith, the former Conservative leader and founder of the Centre for Social Justice, warned that young people were bearing the scars of a divorce 'boom' and a resulting lack of father figures.

'It is a mess, it needs a complete overhaul,' he said. 'It is an organisation locked in secrecy and deeply unhelpful to the parents and the children and all too often able to exacerbate the problems that they are about to face.'

David Laws, the Liberal Democrat children's spokesman, added: 'In too many cases the children become caught up in the crossfire between two warring parties in a system which sometimes encourages the parents to take entrenched positions.'

Miss Davis called for compulsory mediation for parents hoping to use the divorce courts rather than the current 'tick box' exercise for those seeking legal aid.

But a spokesman for the Children's Society said that compulsion 'goes against everything we have learned from many, many years of experience'.

Delyth Morgan, the children's minister, added: 'Divorce and separation can have a devastating impact on children caught in the middle.

'But this survey, looking as far back as 20 years ago, simply doesn't reflect what support is available for families now... we have acted to give families comprehensive counselling, practical and legal support.'

16 November 2009

THE TELEGRAPH

Lone-parent families with young children

Key findings from the Growing Up in Scotland study.

GUS finds that children living in lone-parent households are more likely to experience disadvantage during their early years. However, it is clear that many lone parents are doing the best they can for their children in the face of great difficulties.

⇨ 20% of children aged just under two live in lone-parent families.

⇨ 23% of children aged just under four live in lone-parent families.

⇨ Being a lone parent of children under five is more common among younger mothers and those with low incomes.

20% of children aged just under two live in lone-parent families

⇨ Just under two-thirds of children with a non-resident parent had contact with them, with around half of non-resident parents paying regular maintenance.

⇨ Mothers in couple families are more likely to be employed than lone mothers.

⇨ Lone mothers are more likely than mothers in couple families to have no qualifications.

⇨ Lone-parent families are much more likely than couple families to live in an area of high deprivation.

⇨ Lone-parent families have lower incomes and are much more likely to be dependent on benefits than couple families.

⇨ Lone mothers are less likely than mothers in couple families to attend local groups for parents and children.

⇨ Children in lone-parent households consume a smaller variety of fruit and vegetables than children in couple families.

⇨ Children aged just under four living in lone-parent households were just as likely as those living in couple families to watch TV every day.

⇨ Children in lone-parent families are more likely to have a long-standing illness or disability and to suffer short-term health problems more often than those in couple families.

⇨ Lone parents are more likely than couple parents to express concern about their child's development, learning or behaviour, including speech and language development.

⇨ Lone parents are consistently more likely than couple parents to report that poor heath affects their daily lives.

⇨ Lone parents are less likely to attend antenatal classes and to breastfeed their babies.

October 2008

⇨ The above information is reprinted with kind permission from Growing Up in Scotland. Visit www.crfr.ac.uk/gus for more information.

HEALTH

EMPLOYMENT

QUALIFICATIONS

COMMUNITY

CHILDHOOD DEVELOPMENT

...YOU'RE MISSING A PARENT...

WE'RE MISSING MORE THAN THAT...

CENTRE FOR RESEARCH ON FAMILIES AND RELATIONSHIPS

Single parents bear the brunt of the slump

Charity's helpline goes free.

Single parents have continued to move into work in the past year but the recession is hitting their families hard as fuel and food costs rise, and as working hours and child maintenance payments are cut, warns national charity Gingerbread.

New figures commissioned by the charity show the slightly higher single parent employment rate is limited to those with older children and is not consistent across the country: in the North West, East Midlands and Wales the single parent employment rate dipped between 2008 and 2009.

These figures support preliminary research findings by Gingerbread that suggest that many single parents with older children are trying hard to get jobs in order to avoid new JSA changes that put them at risk of benefit sanctions if they do not seek work.

Rising food and fuel costs inevitably take a bigger bite out of the low weekly budgets of single-parent families (single parents spend over 30 per cent of their budgets on these items) so even those single parents who are able to work are struggling against the slump. Gingerbread's Single Parent Helpline is taking more and more calls from single mums and dads – in and out of work – who are worried about paying the bills.

To reach more of those who need advice or information, the charity is launching a new helpline number – on 0808 802 0925 – which is free to single parents calling from all landlines and all major mobile networks.

Launching the new number and the charity's Recession Briefing today Gingerbread's Chief Executive Fiona Weir said:

'Many single-parent families are facing financial hardship in the recession, not least because fuel and food costs take almost a third of their weekly budget. Parents calling the Gingerbread Single Parent Helpline are saying they are down to the bone. We felt it was important to make calls to the helpline free for all single parents, and from today Gingerbread will pay the cost of the calls.'

Gingerbread is also calling for more Government action to protect vulnerable families during recession. Working with the Campaign to End Child Poverty we are calling for:

⇨ new ways of enabling parents to work in 'short hours jobs' so they can earn more income while working around childcare or school times;

⇨ more investment in child benefit and child tax credit

⇨ more help with the costs of childcare;

⇨ wider entitlements to free school meals.

Fiona Weir, Gingerbread Chief Executive, said:

'Previous recessions have left generations of children blighted by damaging and persistent poverty. It's really important that Government acts to make sure that children in vulnerable families do not bear the brunt of recession again – or society the huge long-term costs that would be the legacy of such a short-sighted approach.'

Key facts from Gingerbread's Recession Briefing:

⇨ Half of single parents are poor and their children are twice as likely to be poor as those in couple families.

⇨ Childcare costs have risen by four per cent from last year.

⇨ Food costs are up four per cent.

⇨ Fuel costs are up eight per cent.

⇨ Low pay and high costs mean one third of children with a working single parent are still poor.

⇨ 70 per cent of single parents surveyed by Gingerbread said they had to go without something for themselves to make ends meet and one-third had to go without something for their children.

⇨ 36 per cent had had to borrow money to stay afloat .

⇨ The overall single parent employment rate went up 0.4 per cent last year to 56.7 per cent but fell slightly for those with younger children. 72 per cent of single parents with a youngest child aged 13 are working compared to 36 per cent of those with a youngest aged two.

⇨ Most single parents can't afford a mortgage and therefore aren't benefiting from lower interest rates.

⇨ Working single parents are usually in part-time, low-paid jobs and face an extra risk of having their hours slashed.

⇨ Only one-third of single parents is getting any child maintenance and in the recession we are hearing from more single parents whose former partner has been laid off and has stopped making the payments for their children.

28 September 2009

⇨ The above information is reprinted with kind permission from Gingerbread. Visit www.gingerbread.org.uk for more information.

© *Gingerbread*

GINGERBREAD

Do grandparents matter?

The impact of grandparenting on the wellbeing of children.

Do grandparents matter?

This timely and important report shows the immense value of grandparents in 21st-century family life. It reveals a unique relationship that exists between the older generation and the youngest: a relationship of love and trust that enables the children to use their grandparents as confidantes and counsellors as well as playmates and cookery instructors.

The report shows that children value the non-critical support, emotional advice and guidance that grandparents offer and enjoy the quality time their grandparents give them. It also found that the relationship has benefits for grandparents, adding to their raison d'être and contributing to their health and longevity.

Family Matters Institute

The report also notes the change in the nature of family relationships in Britain throughout the 20th century, from the extended family to the nuclear family to the current variety of relationships, formal and informal, in which both the elderly and the young suffer neglect.

With today's increased incidence of divorce and family breakdown, grandparents can sometimes provide the only stable family relationship in a child's life, and yet grandparents often lose contact with their grandchildren during or after a divorce or relationship breakup and have no legal rights through the Family Court to continue offering loving care and support to their grandchildren.

The report concludes that there is need for much greater understanding of the role and function of grandparents in family life today.

What makes a good grandparent?

Grandparents are seen as a positive and supportive adult in many children's lives, providing a relationship that is different from that between a child and his or her parents.

Children appreciate the time their grandparents have to spend with them engaging in simple play activities and being 'fun' grandparents, filling a void in the children's lives that their time-limited parents were sometimes unable to address. In contrast, children actively resisted contact with grandparents who sought to function as a surrogate parent, especially in terms of discipline or enforcing values.

Children held expectations of what constituted 'good grandparenting' with kindness, patience and a sense of fun emerging as being highly meaningful for the children. Importantly, from the perspective of the child, the uncritical advocate was the type of grandparent that the children would actively seek out for advice and emotional support.

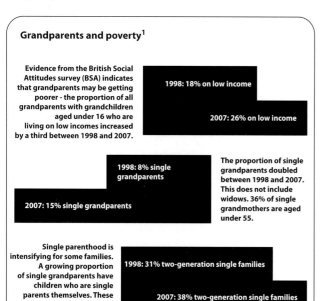

Grandparents and poverty[1]

Evidence from the British Social Attitudes survey (BSA) indicates that grandparents may be getting poorer - the proportion of all grandparents with grandchildren aged under 16 who are living on low incomes increased by a third between 1998 and 2007.

1998: 18% on low income

2007: 26% on low income

1998: 8% single grandparents

2007: 15% single grandparents

The proportion of single grandparents doubled between 1998 and 2007. This does not include widows. 36% of single grandmothers are aged under 55.

Single parenthood is intensifying for some families. A growing proportion of single grandparents have children who are single parents themselves. These families are particularly at risk of financial hardship.

1998: 31% two-generation single families

2007: 38% two-generation single families

Working-age grandmothers on low incomes are most likely to be providing the childcare. They are also more likely to report that they have given up work or reduced their working hours in order to do so and are under the greatest pressure to combine work and care. Additionally, although they are not the poorest grandparents (the poorest are those who are dependent on pension income), they are also the group most likely to report that they are finding it difficult to cope financially, suggesting that it may be the struggle to combine work and care which is significant here.

Notes
1. All statistics quoted here are from the following source: Griggs, J. *The Poor Relation? Grandparental care: where older people's poverty and child poverty meet.* Grandparents Plus, Equality and Human Rights Commission 2009.

Source: Grandparents Plus Policy Briefing Paper - Statistics May 2010. www.grandparentsplus.org.uk

FAMILY MATTERS INSTITUTE

Those children who said that their grandparents were disinterested, critical, or overly strict, expressed feelings of disappointment and loss.

Grandchildren are good for you

Most grandparents regard contact with their grandchildren to be of considerable value, bringing a lot of happiness and a sense of fulfilment into their lives. They enjoy spending time with the children, listening to and sharing in their experiences of school and peer group interaction.

These contacts with the children come to mean a great deal to grandparents who benefit from the joy of watching their grandchildren develop from the cradle to mature young adults.

34% of grandparents give financial help to their grandchildren or support the parents in meeting the cost of bringing up their children

For many of the respondents this contact with the grandchildren gives an additional raison d'être to their lives and therefore becomes a source of great loss and suffering similar to bereavement when family circumstances change and they are denied access to the children.

Practical help

Grandparents can often provide an invaluable source of childcare that enables parents to have a life of their own. 60% of the grandparents in the study were involved in some form of childcare on a regular or occasional basis. 28% regularly care for their grandchildren in the evenings or at nights. Grandparents look after grandchildren while parents are at work; they do school runs – taking or collecting children – and take them to a variety of out-of-school activities. 34% of grandparents give financial help to their grandchildren or support the parents in meeting the cost of bringing up their children.

Grandparents in family breakdown

81% of the grandparents in this study whose children had been involved in family breakdown said they had given support to their grandchildren during times of domestic dispute and the breakup of the parental home. The grandparents often provide the one stable factor in family life and those to whom the children turn for personal counselling and support in times of stress.

Case studies

Ten case studies in the report illustrate the experience of grandparents during times of parental disputes and stress within family life. Many of the grandparents speak of their dismay at discovering that they have no legal rights in offering loving care and support to their grandchildren.

The research

The aim of the research was to examine the role of grandparents in family life today from the perspective of both the children and the grandparents. Two schools participated in the study and a number of organisations working with seniors distributed questionnaires to their members.

The research was carried out jointly by a team from the University of Hertford led by Professor Fiona Brooks and a team from the Family Matters Institute led by Dr Clifford Hill.

You can access the report on the Family Matters website here: www.familymatters.org.uk/doc/Do_Grandparents_Matter_Summary.pdf

May 2009

⇨ The above information is reprinted with kind permission from the Family Matters Institute. Visit www.familymatters.org.uk for more information.

FAMILY MATTERS INSTITUTE

Grandparents not always the most effective childcarers

Many babies who are looked after by grandparents while their mothers are out at work might be better off in nurseries or crèches, a new study suggests.

Grandparents can often help to develop a baby's vocabulary but they may be unable to provide other educational and social experiences that an infant needs, say researchers at the Institute of Education, London.

They have found that children looked after by grandparents at the age of nine months were considered to have more behavioural problems at age three than those who had been in the care of a nursery, crèche, childminder, nanny or another family member. The research involved 4,800 UK children born in 2000 and 2001 who are being tracked by the Millennium Cohort Study. All of the children had mothers who worked when they were babies.

According to their mothers, children who had been cared for by grandparents – more than one in three of those studied – were more likely to have difficult relationships with other youngsters at age three. Boys were said to have particular problems relating to their peers. The behaviour issue affected families of all social backgrounds.

Dr Kirstine Hansen and Dr Denise Hawkes also found that three-year-olds who had been in nurseries and crèches at nine months were often more ready for school than those who had been looked after by grandparents, childminders, family members or friends. On average, they achieved higher scores in an assessment that measured their understanding of colours, letters, numbers, sizes, comparisons and shapes.

> **Grandparents can often help to develop a baby's vocabulary but they may be unable to provide other educational and social experiences that an infant needs, say researchers**

However, children with highly educated mothers tended to have more extensive vocabularies if they had been looked after by a grandparent – the maternal grandmother in most cases. Grandparents also had a positive effect on the vocabularies of children living in two-parent families, those with older mothers and those in families that were not claiming benefits.

'This may, of course, reflect the better vocabulary skills of grandmothers in such families,' says Dr Hansen, research director of the Millennium Cohort Study. 'But it may also be partly because grandparents talk to children more than other carers, not only because they have more time, but because they compensate for a reduction in physical activities with the child.

'There is also evidence that older people are more likely to use grammatically correct sentences and speak more slowly to children. They are also less likely to tolerate grammatical errors and will correct their grandchildren's language.'

The study did not investigate why children looked after by grandparents appear to exhibit more behavioural problems. But the researchers point out that some previous studies suggest pre-school settings such as nurseries can help children to develop the social skills they need to get on with their peers. 'Children who are looked after by grandparents, on the other hand, spend more time with adults,' they add.

However, the researchers argue that grandparent childcarers deserve support rather than criticism. 'Our research shows that grandparent care contributes both positively and negatively to child outcomes, and perhaps with Government support this situation could be improved,' they say.

There are currently no allowances, tax breaks or grants for grandparents who care for grandchildren. If grandparents register as child minders they can receive support and training and can be paid by the parent who can claim back some of the cost through Working Tax Credit. However, at present, grandparents can only do this if they also care for a child who is not a relative.

'Understandably, many grandparents are unable or unprepared to take on this additional burden,' Dr Hansen says. 'Perhaps a more flexible approach which offers training and support for informal carers should be considered rather than encouraging them down the formal care routes. It should be possible for grandparents to receive recognition and reward for the caring they are already doing.'

The study also found that girls appeared to benefit especially from time spent in nurseries and crèches, as did children from two-parent families and those with better-educated mothers. However, children with younger mothers and those living in households claiming benefits were also found to be more ready for school if they had attended nurseries or crèches.

'This is almost certainly because nurseries and crèches are more likely to offer structure and content to daily activities with children and their staff are more likely to be trained, to have better facilities and resources and to provide more educational stimulation,' the researchers say. 'This is another of the study's important findings because it suggests that this form of childcare has the potential to reduce inequalities.

'Our study therefore delivers a reassuring message for the UK Government, which has invested a great deal in policies that are aimed at improving child outcomes and reducing the achievement gap between advantaged and disadvantaged families.'

The study's findings will be reported in an article, 'Early childcare and child development', that will appear in the forthcoming issue of the *Journal of Social Policy*, published by Cambridge University Press. The online version of the article can be accessed via the CUP website journals.cambridge.org/jsp/childcare from today (February 10).

10 February 2009

⇨ This information appears as a press release on the IOE website here: www.ioe.ac.uk/newsEvents/16093. html. It is reprinted with the permission of the Institute of Education (University of London). The study's findings are reported in an article, 'Early childcare and child development', from the *Journal of Social Policy*, published by Cambridge University Press. The online version of the article can be accessed via the CUP website: www. journals.cambridge.org/jsp/childcare

© *Institute of Education, University of London*

Grandparents and childcare

Families with grandparent childcarers - 1 in 3

1 in 3 families depend on grandparents for childcare[1].

Single parents with grandparents childcarers - 47%

Half (47%) of single parents depend on grandparents for childcare[2].

£££ The value of the grandparental childcare contribution has been calculated at £3.9billion[3].

Parents turning to grandparents for childcare - 4 in 10

4 out of 10 parents say they are more likely to turn to grandparents for extra help with childcare during the recession[4].

Children cared for by grandparents are thought to be less 'school ready' than those in formal childcare settings[5].

Mothers in professional/managerial roles using formal childcare - 6 in 10

Mothers in unskilled/semi-skilled jobs using formal childcare - 1 in 20

Over 6 out of 10 (64%) mothers working in professional and managerial roles use formal childcare compared to just 1 in 20 (6%) mothers in unskilled and semi-skilled jobs. Half of mothers in low-paid work rely on grandparents for childcare[6].

Grandparents under 54 providing childcare often - 45%

Grandparents 65-74 providing childcare often - 25%

Almost half (45%) of grandparents aged under 54 are providing childcare 'often' compared to 1 in 4 (25%) of those aged 65-74[7].

Notes
1. Office for National Statistics, *Social Trends*, April 2009.
2. Bell, A et al *A question of balance, lone parents, childcare and work*. Department for Work and Pensions Research Report 230, 2005.
3. *The Economy of Older People*, Age Concern, 2004.
4. Grandparents Plus, YouGov survey February 2009.
5. Hanson, K and Hawkes, D. *Journal of Social Policy*, Cambridge University Press, 38 p211-239, February 2009.
6. Dex, S and Ward K. *Parental care and employment in early childhood*. Analysis of the Millennium Cohort Study, 2007.
7. Griggs, J. *The Poor Relation? Grandparental care: where older people's poverty and child poverty meet*. Grandparents Plus, Equality and Human Rights Commission 2009.

Source: Grandparents Plus Policy Briefing Paper - Statistics May 2010. www.grandparentsplus.org.uk

INSTITUTE OF EDUCATION, UNIVERSITY OF LONDON

Thinking of adopting

Information from After Adoption.

What is adoption?

Adoption is a lifelong commitment. It's about providing a permanent family for a child or children in care who cannot, for whatever reason, return home. When you adopt a child, you take on all the rights and responsibilities for the child that the birth parent had. It's the stability and security of family life that makes it such a positive option for children.

Can I adopt?

Your application will be welcomed if you are over 21 and you can provide a permanent, stable and caring home. Remember that nearly everyone who completes the adoption process – 94% – is recommended to adopt.

What sort of person do you have to be?

All sorts of people can make a success of adoption. It doesn't matter whether you are married or single, in or out of work, or whatever your race, religion or sexuality.

Above all, you need to be determined to give a young person the sort of support that will really make a difference to their lives.

Is there anyone who can't adopt?

There are very few people who can't adopt. Anyone who has committed certain serious criminal offences, including crimes against children or violent offences, will not be able to adopt.

Which children need adopting?

There are all sorts of children who need adoptive parents, from toddlers to teenagers. It is rare, however, for babies to come up for adoption. Sometimes there are two, three or more brothers and sisters who need to live and grow up together.

Some children may have been abused or neglected in their past. Other children may have physical or learning disabilities. The one thing all these children have in common is that their parents are unable to care for them and they need a new, permanent family to care for them as they grow up.

Who do I talk to if I want to adopt?

You need to contact an adoption agency such as Families that Last. This will either be the adoption team in your local authority, or an approved voluntary adoption agency. Contact Families that Last on 0161 819 3108 and we will be pleased to answer your questions about what happens, the child who needs adopting and so on.

What happens next?

There are several steps to go through after you first contact an adoption agency. The first steps include preparation for you as an adoptive parent and assessment by the agency.

Remember, this process is a two-way partnership. It's a chance for you to think everything through and for the agency to find out a lot more about you. During this period you can expect to:

⇨ Meet adoptive parents and social workers to find out about adoption first-hand;

⇨ Have your questions about adoption answered;

⇨ Be seen by a social worker in your own home;

⇨ Be asked detailed questions about your own background and circumstances.

The preparation and assessment process is lengthy, but this is for very good reasons. From the agency's point of view, adoption is for life and it is important that they make sure the adoptive parents they approve are the right ones. But adoption is also a major decision for you. The assessment gives you an opportunity to take an honest look at what you want out of adoption and what you can give. You need to be certain at the end of it, that you want to make a lifetime commitment.

What happens after assessment?

At the end of the assessment period, a report goes forward to an adoption panel – a group of social workers, other professionals and independent people. Based on their recommendation, the adoption agency will then decide whether or not to approve you as a prospective adoptive parent. Once approved, the agency will begin to match you to a suitable child. In some cases an agency may already have children in mind and this process would start earlier.

How long does it all take?

New standards for adoption say the entire process, from your initial phone call, to being approved as a prospective adoptive parent, should take no more than eight months. All adoption agencies are working towards this goal.

Once you are approved, the process of matching you to a suitable child can take from a couple of weeks to over a year. Things are changing in adoption to help speed this up. The new adoption register allows adoption agencies to link adoptive parents with children waiting to be adopted, so you and the children who need new homes don't have to wait so long.

AFTER ADOPTION

How is an adoption made legal?

Some time after the child comes to live with you, the court will make an Adoption Order. An Adoption Order ends all legal ties the child has with the birth family. The child takes your surname and becomes a full member of your family.

What rights do birth parents have after the adoption?

Once an Adoption Order has been made, the birth parents have no legal rights over the child and cannot claim him or her back.

Will the child still see their birth parents or other relatives?

The child may well benefit from continuing to see (or to have letter contact with), other important people in their lives. It will depend on the child, but this could be a birth parent, foster carer who has looked after them for a long time, brothers or sisters, grandparents or other relatives. If they have made strong attachments, it can really help the child to keep these up. This is something your adoption agency will discuss with you before a child comes to live with you.

Will I be told about the child's background?

It is very important that you know as much as possible about the child's past. The law says the adoption agency must give you information about the child, which includes details about his or her background, time in care, school history and any medical needs. This knowledge will help you understand the child when they come to live with you, help the child understand the circumstances of their adoption and help you find the best way of supporting them in the future.

Will I be paid?

You are expected to meet the general living costs of a child you adopt like any parent. However, you may be able to get an Adoption Allowance, which is means-tested and depends on the needs of the child. You may also be entitled to benefits – speak to your social worker or local benefits agency.

What support will I get from the agency after adopting?

In the first few years, it is ideal for you to continue to work in partnership with the agency so that the child gets the best possible start as part of your family. When you first contact the agency, ask them about support offered after the adoption.

What other support will I get?

Advice and support is available to all adoptive families, not just at the time of adoption but in the months and years to follow. Families that Last is a project of After Adoption.

Sometimes the best form of support comes from other adoptive parents. After Adoption can put you in touch with groups of local adoptive parents who are in the same situation and understand the issues. Visit www. afteradoption.org.uk

⇨ Extract from information provided by After Adoption: www.afteradoption.org.uk. Reprinted with permission.

© After Adoption

Key facts about adoption

Information from After Adoption.

⇨ One in four people in the UK have an adoption connection – adoption is part of the fabric of modern family life.

⇨ There were approximately 65,000 children in care in England and Wales at the end of March 2005, of which around only 40 per cent will return home.

⇨ It is estimated that just one per cent of children in care go on to university – a statistic that has huge knock-on effects for society as a whole.

⇨ People who have been in care are 66 times more likely to have their own children taken into care.

⇨ Only 4,000 children were adopted during the year ending March 2005 and just 210 of these children were under age one.

⇨ The average age at which children are adopted is four years and two months.

⇨ The Adoption and Children Act 2002 (enforced December 2005) was the first piece of adoption legislation in over a quarter of a century. The Act gave unmarried and same-sex couples the right to jointly adopt.

⇨ The Act also gave birth relatives the right to request that their local authority or relevant adoption society make contact with their birth children, provided they are over 18 and are happy to be contacted.

⇨ After Adoption runs TALKadoption, the only UK-wide helpline for young people that focuses specifically on adoption issues.

⇨ Information provided by After Adoption: www. afteradoption.org.uk. Reprinted with permission.

© After Adoption

AFTER ADOPTION

The best thing we've ever done

Carol and Tony think they've got a normal family, full of normal ups and downs – with a daughter who just 'happens' to be adopted! They tell Sophie Offord about the tears, the laughter, and the support that pulls them through.

'If I speak to people who have no idea about her background, I say the word "adopted", but it doesn't feel like it's needed: she just feels like my daughter.' Tony smiles and shrugs: 'It just feels like "family"'.

The 'family' I am speaking to is made up of Tony and Carol, their adopted daughter, Cassie, 12, and a couple of children from Carol's previous relationship, Plaxy, 29, and Jamie, 22: long grown up and moved out but still 'coming and going' on a regular basis.

'I suppose our family is atypical in some ways,' says Carol. 'I'm white British, Tony is black Jamaican, and Cassie is white British and black African-American, so we're a mixed-race family. I've been married before. But all this is normal for many families these days!'

> **'If I speak to people who have no idea about her background, I say the word "adopted", but it doesn't feel like it's needed: she just feels like my daughter'**

In fact, Carol and Tony are proof that you can be an older parent, in your forties or even fifties, and still be able to adopt, depending on the needs and age of the child. And you don't have to be rich or living a life of leisure. Carol and Tony work full time – Carol as a special needs teacher and Tony as a dental technician. It seems like the couple have always led a busy life, both socially and professionally – so what drew them to adoption in the first place?

'We were sitting down with a glass of wine one evening,' recalls Carol, 'Talking about where our lives were going as a couple. We decided that we would get married and build a family life together, possibly through adoption.'

'The next time I went into school, I saw a pile of leaflets about adoption in reception. It was like they were sitting there, waiting for us. I took them home, got in touch with the agency, and here we are now!'

Carol and Tony's experience of the adoption process is a positive one. 'It was all relatively stress-free and simple. We didn't have a long searching process, which

I know is unusual. On the day we went to the panel to be approved, our social worker told us about a potentially suitable child – which was Cassie.'

Carol continues: 'We were sent the "papers" on Cassie, which told us lots of information about her, but we did ask to see papers of other children too. It's a bit like buying a dress: if you like the first one you see and you haven't compared, how do you know it's right? Not that I'm comparing you to a dress, Cassie!' Cassie, who has been sitting at the table in the garden with us, rolls her eyes playfully. Her mum pulls her closer: 'But in the end, you just felt right, like you were meant to be here!'

Carol and Tony insist that nothing is kept from Cassie about her adoption, and she seems to love listening to these stories of how she found her 'forever family'. She doesn't say much, but grins shyly, her big, brown eyes full of twinkles. Especially when Carol tells the story of their introduction…

'I think that it was one of the most magical times in our lives – that week of anticipation, between Christmas and New Year, which we spent meeting Cassie. There were hundreds of miles of travel, with the radio playing in the car, driving to and from her foster home in Kent. On January 6th, she finally came to live with us.'

Carol and Tony always celebrate that day now, usually by doing what they did the first day she moved in – going to the water garden centre to look at the fishes there.

'It's getting boring now,' pipes up Cassie, breaking her silence. 'I'd rather have a big party!' Carol and Cassie spend a few moments working out how long it's been since she joined them and a compromise emerges: Cassie will get a party, but only when the anniversary clocks in at ten years! This isn't all that far away, I remind them…

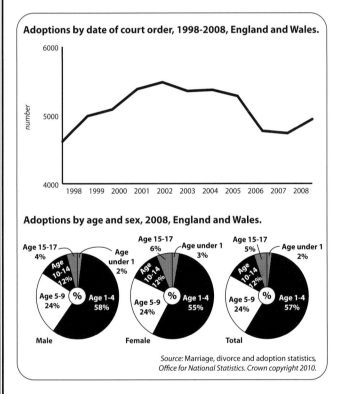

Adoptions by date of court order, 1998-2008, England and Wales.

Adoptions by age and sex, 2008, England and Wales.

Male
Age 15-17 4%
Age 10-14 12%
Age under 1 2%
Age 5-9 24%
Age 1-4 58%

Female
Age 15-17 6%
Age under 1 3%
Age 10-14 12%
Age 5-9 24%
Age 1-4 55%

Total
Age 15-17 5%
Age under 1 2%
Age 10-14 12%
Age 5-9 24%
Age 1-4 57%

Source: Marriage, divorce and adoption statistics, Office for National Statistics. Crown copyright 2010.

For Cassie is now nearly a teenager, with a busy after-school life that revolves around things like Guides and singing lessons. Halfway through my chat with Carol and Tony, she leaps up to leave the table, realising she is running late for choir! Meanwhile, Carol's birth children are adults in their own right, working and travelling and getting on with things independently.

'Cassie is like an only child now, and I sometimes wonder if she might have thrived in an adoptive family with lots of other children – but we'll never know. She's had a different experience. She's had our undivided attention, which she has probably needed.' Carol and Tony go on to tell me about some of Cassie's difficulties. She can display challenging behaviours, and needs help with some emotional, social and academic needs.

Carol says she has drawn from her years as a special needs teacher – and a parent. Just as every family is different, every child is different too, needing and thriving on different things. Not every prospective adopter needs previous parenting or childcare experience, but Carol has found it invaluable. 'I think it's why I've found everything a bit easier than Tony. It's still the hardest thing I've ever done – but it's also the best thing.' 'Yes, this is my first experience of having a child,' says Tony. 'And it's been… interesting.' They both burst out laughing at his diplomacy.

Carol and Tony's advice to prospective families is straight to the point – don't rule yourself out. No, it's not for everyone, they say: but for those with the drive and willingness to adopt, all you need is the right support.

Carol and Tony haven't liked baring their soul, but agree that they've benefited from social work and professional involvement. Both have attended sessions at the Post-Adoption Centre and gone on lots of training courses. Good friends are crucial too – whether or not they have personal experience of adoption. Feeling supported is imperative, wherever it comes from.

'Don't feel inadequate,' pleads Tony, as if the prospective adoptive family is right there in front of him. 'Needing support doesn't make you a failure. Love is not enough.'

Yet it is clear that Carol and Tony are united in their love for Cassie. I am barely out of the door and the couple are already discussing the coming weekend, with Cassie very much at the centre of events. The couple tell me that they have loved her from the very first time they saw her.

'I know it sounds odd,' laughs Carol, 'But I can imagine how she was as a baby – as if I've had that experience, as if I've got the memories! It just feels like she is ours, like we've had her from the beginning.'

So would they do it all over again? 'It's not been an easy ride, but adopting has been so worthwhile.' Tony leans back in his chair and radiates happiness: 'Oh, you feel so fantastic. Sometimes, if I'm at work, and things get busy, I think about home and some of the things Cassie says that make me laugh. Or the night she lay in my arms and asked me to show her the difference between left and right – to think that for ever and ever she'll remember that her daddy was the one who showed her. It's all those little moments. I never thought that something like this would happen in my life. We both feel so lucky.'

BAAF

The rise of the gay dad

Having two dads isn't as unusual as it used to be. Rebecca Seal meets the generation of young, gay men who are re-inventing the world of adoption.

More and more children are being adopted by same-sex couples. In the past two years the number of gay men approved to adopt has doubled. Here we listen to some of their stories.

Peter, 44, and his partner adopted brothers Carlos, eight, and PJ, four

You never know what prejudices you will come across. If you approach an agency about a child or sibling group, they are at liberty to say you don't match the profiles of these children, and you hear nothing from them and you don't know why that is. Even at the recruitment stage, you might hear agencies saying they've already got a gay or lesbian couple on their books and they're not looking for any more, or because you're white you can't go on their books, or because you're gay you'll not get children under five. It isn't an even playing field. But maybe that will change when social workers have more experience of kids doing just as well in gay- or lesbian-headed households.

The statistics from the National Adoption Register suggest gay and lesbian adopters are more open to older kids and sibling groups, and also we're more ethnically mixed as couples than heterosexuals. We represent a different profile of adopters. And being gay or lesbian should help you relate to the experiences of these children, because they've experienced difficult starts in life, they feel different and excluded and aware that other children haven't had similar experiences.

There are a lot of very supportive, well-meaning social workers. But sometimes they can impose a hierarchy of adopters in which married heterosexual adopters with money are at the top and a single, gay, white man would be at the bottom – a single, gay, black man would be higher, since they are keen to match ethnically (most gay and lesbian adopters think they were never going to have children who were going to look like them anyway, so what does it matter?). The law is just about giving gay and lesbian adopters an equal opportunity to apply.

I don't necessarily disagree with lots of stereotypes about gay people – it's the way that they are used to suggest that we are less worthy as parents that's the problem. There's still a heterosexist attitude, where everything straight is seen as better because it's the norm.

You spend months talking to your child's social worker, and to the family-finder whose job it is to match you. We only saw one picture of the boys and read a 200-word profile to begin with – although as it gets closer you get huge documents and masses of files. Then you might first get to meet their foster carer, or a birth relative who is positively inclined towards the adoption. Next, you might get to meet the child for an hour one day, and the next day a whole morning, then the next day you might put them to bed or take them to the park. So over time you get to know them – maybe a few days if they are small and a month if they're older, and there's a transition where they begin to understand who is responsible for their care. Ours was over 12 days. Our boys attached to us very quickly and it was lovely, a really beautiful time.

> **More and more children are being adopted by same-sex couples. In the past two years the number of gay men approved to adopt has doubled**

We're lucky to be in a school with other children with gay and lesbian parents. I think it is more difficult for people who don't have that, as school very much becomes your world. We know lots of kids who've got a dad and a stepdad. When other kids visit they might think: 'Oh, your two dads live together', but I don't think our kids even see us as different, and other kids don't seem to notice.

It's a challenging thing taking on children of a certain age – they've got histories and attitudes and experiences and friends and attachments to people they might not see again. Most people try to give their children the sense that, notionally at least, their birth parents did love them even if they weren't cut out for parenting.

Paul is 49 and has been with his partner Matt, 41, for 19 years. They adopted brothers Harry, eight, and David, six

My partner and I talked about adopting one night after we'd had our civil partnership ceremony. We'd been together 15 years and were thinking about what we could do that might help someone. We were so naive – we didn't know who we could adopt or foster; we thought perhaps we could only foster a child of, say, 12, who

THE GUARDIAN

was in difficulty for six months or something. Then we started to discover we could be taken seriously as adopters. We were told that often it's harder for a child to be adopted if they are older, that if they are sibling groups they're often at the end of the queue, waiting. It began to get quite heart-wrenching.

It took nearly three and a half years for us to adopt. The day we first met our boys was a shell shock. I remember naively asking about what happens if it doesn't go well and they're not the right ones – do we choose again? And the adoption staff said: 'No, no, no – we've found the boys, you've all agreed that this might be a good match, it's happening, there's no going back. These are the ones.' We went to the foster home with real trepidation – and because it was a foster home I had this vision of it being a run-down old house and lots of kids and a maternal lady in a pinafore. It was actually an immaculate house. We went up to this glass door and although we'd seen pictures of the boys we had no idea what they were really like, and there they were jumping up at the door, like puppies. They were two stunning little boys, just fantastic. It's a really artificial set-up of course, manufactured by the social workers, who say you'll have a cup of tea and you'll get to talk to them, but you mustn't pick them up, give them space, don't get too close. But it was a great three-quarters of an hour. And afterwards in the car, I said to my partner: 'Let's not make too big a thing of this,' and he looked at me and said: 'You're joking? This is huge.' We just knew as soon as we went in that it was going to work.

There was a lot of prejudice in the adoption system, even though it's not allowed and the law states you must treat everyone the same and with respect. There are still individuals who have difficulty getting over the fact that their values and mindset don't fit with what they have to do in their job. And now there's clearly prejudice when people realise the set-up. There's what I call the mummy prejudice – the boys misbehave in public and one of us dads will berate that child, and you get a clear sense from groups of women out with their kids that they think once those boys get home their mum will sort it out. And I'm thinking: it doesn't work like that!

People are quite innocent too – my children are darker-skinned than me, so people often ask if they are my kids and I'll say yes, and they'll go: 'Oh. How come?' And this will be in front of the boys.

Their school is absolutely brilliant. It's the first time they've had adopted children with same-sex parents, and they're very sweet – they take you to one side and say: 'What should we do on Mother's Day?' We say they can make a card if they want to – although someone did once say: 'But they haven't got a mother.' To which I responded: 'Well, how do you think they got here?'

Times have changed immensely: I put myself forward to be a governor and I got voted in by the parents who know all about me, which is fantastic, because I'm old enough to remember being too scared to ever tell anyone I was gay.

People focus too much on the fact that two men can't have a child. But what they forget is that adoption is not about starting a child – it's about taking over and parenting damaged children, and that's a skill. I'm not putting us up on a pedestal. All I'm saying is that we're a real resource.

Zoltan, 38, and Mark, 35, have been together for 11 years and officially adopted five-year-old Lucia two weeks ago

Zoltan: I was fostered myself and I wanted to give something back, as it were, and Mark has a really magical quality with children. Kids just feel really comfortable with him. At first we wanted to foster. We went through the fostering approval processes, and our very first placement was two little girls, half-sisters Natalie and Lucia. After a while it became clear that they were never going to go back to their mother and so, two and a half years after she was placed with us, Lucia is now our daughter. The initial plan was for them to be adopted together, by us. But in the end Natalie's real father wanted her (he's not Lucia's father).

The local authority was very pro us adopting, but we did have difficulties trying to foster. Once you're approved to foster you go on a list, and when social workers have

THE GUARDIAN

an urgent or planned child to place they go down the list and start phoning people. Five or six times we had false starts – we'd be told a child was arriving and then it didn't happen. I got suspicious, because we were the only male, same-sex couple registered in the borough. It got to a point where we were supposed to be doing respite care with two boys in foster care, and we think their biological family vetoed us, even though the children had been removed from them. So I said to the authority: 'You need to assess what your policies are, because this looks like homophobia.' I was very tough and a week later, Lucia and Natalie arrived.

The first social worker who came to assess us said: 'Would I want my child to be adopted by two gay men? I don't know…' and then she went: 'I think I would.' And that was her mind made up.

The first adoption panel was a bizarre experience. The maximum number of people on the panel is 15, but, perhaps because we were the only male same-sex couple in the borough, there were 17.

The whole process is in some ways fantastically well thought out and set up: you're assigned a social worker and there's one for the child, plus independent legal representatives who are supposed to represent the children. That's good, but the risk is that people have different ideas and agendas; we felt that one of the legal representatives was homophobic.

The kids in Lucia's class know everything, and there are other children with same-sex parents too. Kids will come up to us and say: 'So you're Lucia's daddy?' Yes. 'And she's got two daddies?' Yes. 'Why?' And then another one says: 'Cos her mummy's poorly.' It's great. The school has been so supportive – they asked what they could do and who they could write to, and when we told the headmistress two weeks ago she was in tears.

Mark: Sometimes the stress and pressure became immense – we both stormed out at times. But Zoltan's my whole life and we're as solid as a rock. We'd been together nine years when we started this. In Lucia's eyes we're Daddy Markie and Daddy Zoltie. She's very assertive – if I'm helping at her school I'll be surrounded by kids and she'll come pushing through them, saying: 'That's my daddy.' Lucia's been with us throughout this process, remember, and she's been overwhelmed by it, I think. She's had a lot of uncertainty, and you forget how much they pick up. But two weeks ago we were finally able to say: 'You are now our daughter.' She got straight on the phone to my mum and says: 'Right, Nan, now I'm adopted, what we're going to do is sort my bedroom out,' and off they went and bought new curtains.

Simon, 36, and his partner have been together for 12 years. They adopted David when he was six, two years ago

Our adoption was very smooth. We started the process in 2006 and it took us about 18 months to get approved and then about six months to actually find our son. He moved in with us two years ago. We were the first gay couple to go through the process in our area, and our local authority gave us so much support. We live in a small village and they've all been good too – we've always been very open, and they knew from day one what we were doing and were more curious than anything.

At first he called us by our first names. Now he calls us Dad and Daddy – I'm Dad, James is Daddy. I think that'll peter out – he won't want to call James Daddy when he's 16. It came naturally that he called me Dad because, as I like to put it, I had my maternity leave, so I was off work for nine months and with him all the time; James was there evenings and weekends.

There's always going to be a degree of prejudice about gay adoption. But these children have come from incredibly bad backgrounds – what they've experienced in the early parts of their lives an adult would find very hard to cope with. These children have one or two loving parents – someone who loves them, who'll give them cuddles. Whether they're a gay or straight couple or a single person, as long as the child is getting support it doesn't matter. The odd person in the village said they weren't sure about what we were doing – that a child needed a mummy and a daddy – and I agree. But when that's not available, there's the next best thing.

Adoption orders by date of court order, by whether child born within/outside marriage, 1998-2008, England and Wales.

Adoption orders by date of court order, by sex and whether child born within/outside marriage, 2008, England and Wales.

Source: Marriage, divorce and adoption statistics, ONS. Crown copyright 2010.

THE GUARDIAN

Rodney, 41, is single and adopted Sebastian, four, in January

There are very few men who adopt on their own. I wanted children but never met the right person to do it with. Normally single men who adopt are men who've worked with kids, or who know a particular child and then adopt them. It's quite rare to adopt like me, just because you want to have a child, although it is happening more and more. My agency had never had a single gay guy adopt. I've since been approved to have another child under two, but there are some difficulties. I'm finding it hard to get the authorities to believe that a single gay man is fully capable of bringing up more than one child.

Probably the weirdest thing was that once they've made the match and approved you, you start the process of getting to know the child by making a little storybook about yourself and a DVD of yourself, and the house and your car and their new toys and their room, where they might eat and so on, and they might watch that every day for a week, so they've got a bit of an idea of what to expect. Because I'm single I got a friend to help me, and I pretended that a stuffed giraffe was showing him round the house – it had to be age-appropriate and he was three. He called me Daddy from the start. Lots of tears – it was an incredibly emotional time. My best friend went through the process with me – to have someone at every stage was something I really needed – and then my sister moved over from Australia for 18 months to help. Plus the agency was very clear that I needed a strong support network.

The funniest thing is that 99% of people tell me how lucky Sebastian is, but I feel like the luckiest person in the world. People think we adopters are all doing something great, but it's the best thing I've ever done.

Guy, 31, and Richard, 32, have been together eight years and are in the process of adopting

Guy: We both always knew we wanted children. We did look into surrogacy very briefly and quickly realised that it was incredibly complicated and expensive, and also knowing that there are children out there who need homes, we didn't feel comfortable with going through all that effort.

As with any couple talking about having kids, you always think: 'One day, one day', but now we're really going through the steps. It's a big jump. We bought a house and as soon as we'd fixed it up, we were like: we're ready.

I'm relatively young, so I don't really know anyone else doing this. Until we joined support groups we didn't know any gay couples who have kids, although we have a few friends who are gay couples and are thinking about the same things, or about artificial insemination or surrogacy. In our support group there are older men adopting who 15 years ago found it was impossible. But still, we definitely feel like pioneers.

Richard: There is a certain lifestyle that people associate with gay men rather than gay women. It's not something I've ever identified with. That 'Queer as Folk' lifestyle. There are some great representations of same-sex relationships, but things are often tarnished with that brush of being wild and noncommittal and brash. So it's nice to meet men who have taken that same step of wanting to or actually having kids. It's also generational. Older couples are now out of the closet – my friends have gay neighbours who are in their 60s who have been together 25 years. Ten years ago you wouldn't have seen that – they would have kept a lower profile. But nowadays you realise it's a valid choice and, no, you don't have to go out in Old Compton Street every night.

We are very early on in the process – we have made calls and enquiries, read books and talked about it for a long time, and we just had our first informal meeting with a social worker. Last week they said they would take us on and assess us. Next it's the approval process, which involves six to nine months of meetings, reports and statements from friends, prep groups, and then you hopefully get matched with a child, then there's another panel that makes sure the match is a match. This can take a lot longer for same-sex couples because the kids' social workers can sometimes disregard you in a way they wouldn't disregard others.

However, the available kids are usually black or of dual heritage, so we as a white couple can't really help them out. Most problems have been because we are Caucasian rather than both being male. I think this, in part, is because people can no longer express any homophobia directly, as it's so against their policies now. I think a lot of the local authorities are under more pressure to recruit same-sex adopters. So it's actually a positive time to do it.

Ideally we would like two children, and that also helps in terms of age range. Babies are rare. Aged two to five is the most competitive area, and there you are competing with more conventional couples. So we are open to most ages. There is such a vast difference between the ages, and it's hard to know if you don't actually have kids. At the start of everything, there are a lot of questions about what you would like and want and will or won't accept, and I find it quite surprising, as you just don't know. You are talking about individuals. An eight-year-old needs a home as much as a four-year-old.

The children's names have been changed.
25 October 2009

Nearly a third of young men live with their parents

Nearly a third of men and a fifth of women aged 20 to 34 live with their parents, the Office for National Statistics reports today.

Figures published in the annual ONS 'state of the nation' report *Social Trends* show that, in the second quarter of 2008, 29 per cent of 20- to 34-year-old men and 18 per cent of women of the same age lived with their parents. This equated to around 1.8 million men and 1.1 million women.

Social Trends, which this year takes the theme of households, families and children, also shows that the greatest proportion of this age group living with their parents was aged 20 to 24. In 2008 more than half (52 per cent) of men aged 20 to 24 and more than a third (37 per cent) of women lived with their parents.

Since 2001, the number of 20- to 34-year-olds living at the parental home has increased by nearly 300,000. In 2001, the proportion of young adults living at home stood at 27 per cent of 20- to 34-year-old men and 15 per cent of women in the same age group.

Part of the reason for the increase in the number of young people living with their parents may be that more young adults are continuing their studies after compulsory education.

Over the past four decades the number of students in higher education in the UK has quadrupled, rising from 621,000 in 1970/71 to more than 2.5 million in 2006/07.

Another factor may be that the unemployment rate is higher for people aged 16 to 24 than for older people.

In the second quarter of 2008, 20 per cent of 16- to 24-year-olds in the UK with dependent children and 13 per cent without dependent children were unemployed. This compares with six per cent of people with dependent children and four per cent of people without dependent children aged 25 to 34 and three per cent of people with and without dependent children aged between 50 and state pension age.

According to a Eurobarometer survey in 2007, the most common reasons given by young adults in Europe for why young people live with their parents were that they couldn't afford to move out or that there wasn't enough affordable housing available.

Around four in ten (38 per cent) people in the UK aged 15 to 30 believed that the main reason young adults lived with their parents was because they couldn't afford

to move out and around four in ten (44 per cent) felt it was because of a lack of affordable housing.

For the EU-27 countries as a whole, a higher proportion of respondents (44 per cent) believed young adults couldn't afford to move out than in the UK but a smaller proportion (28 per cent) felt there was a lack of affordable housing.

Around one in eight (12 per cent) 15- to 30-year-olds in the UK felt the main reason young adults stayed at home was because they wanted the comforts at home without the responsibilities. In the EU-27 countries as a whole this figure was around one in six (16 per cent).

15 April 2009

⇨ The above information is reprinted with kind permission from the Office for National Statistics. Visit www.statistics.gov.uk for more information.

OFFICE FOR NATIONAL STATISTICS

Today's young adults can't afford to let go

Bryony Gordon is a 'Yuckie' – Young Unwitting Costly Kid. She asks why so many adults are still being funded by mum and dad.

My name is Bryony and I am a Yuckie. It's not quite the word I wanted to use to describe myself, but there it is, the latest acronym trotted out to denote what I am: a Young Unwitting Costly Kid, sapping my baby-boomer parents of all their hard-earned savings, and probably their will to live. New research released this week has found that an incredible 93 per cent of parents contribute to the finances of their Yuckies.

Previously I have been a Kipper – Kids In Parents' Pockets Eroding Retirement Savings – while other members of my generation – I think that we are Generation Y, or perhaps I; one can never quite be sure – have been described as boomerang kids, returning to live at home when they really should know better.

Anyway, silly names aside, I am still partly reliant on my parents despite being old enough to be one myself, a point that my mother never tires of making. 'You know that you are going to be 30 this year,' she says. 'When I was your age, I was already paying your school fees.'

Gosh, my school fees. What a waste of money that was. Here I am, no more a home-owner than I am a trapeze artist or for that matter a circus elephant, one toe clinging desperately to the very bottom rung of the property ladder thanks only to my mother who bought most of the flat that I live in. Last month she had to pay my gas bill.

And I am not alone. There's my friend Tom, traipsing around Ikea with his mum to furnish the studio flat he can sort of afford to rent ('this was not what I had in mind,' he says). Some Yuckies look further ahead. One acquaintance – let's call her Sue – tells me she lies awake thinking of ways to kill off her in-laws, who she believes are currently blowing her husband's inheritance on a three-week tour of Australia. She's joking, I think.

> **Abbey Mortgages research found that in 2009, almost 500,000 adults aged between 35 and 44 returned home to live with their parents, while 440,000 25- to 34-year-olds did so**

Earlier this week, I found myself talking to an exasperated colleague whose 34-year-old son had moved back in. That morning he had complained when they ran out of milk.

These cases may sound pitiful but they are by no means isolated. Abbey Mortgages research found that in 2009, almost 500,000 adults aged between 35 and 44 returned home to live with their parents, while 440,000 25- to 34-year-olds did so. The Abbey research, published at the end of last year, found that parents of boomerang kids had typically withdrawn about a fifth of their savings to pay for them, but the most recent figures, published earlier this week by the Children's Mutual, found that a third of parents are remortgaging their homes to raise the £30,000 needed to keep their Yuckies.

It is a grim picture, isn't it? No wonder baby boomers are now being labelled the baby gloomers, their pensions – ha! Imagine having a pension! – being used to finance the monthly commute to work of their first born, and very possibly the costs of care for their own parents, as opposed to a happy, relaxed retirement.

Well, tough, I say. For statistics uncovered by David Willetts, the Shadow University and Skills Secretary,

---

Research from The Children's Mutual was undertaken among 1,484 parents of children aged 18 and over. Findings include:

Parents who will have to retire later – 57%

57 per cent of parents of 18- to 30-year-olds say they have no choice but to retire later, with four in ten (43 per cent) expecting to work up to five years longer than they wanted because of the cost of their 'adult' children.

Parent with three children unable to retire – 8%

Parent with four children unable to retire – 14%

Eight per cent of parents with three children say they won't be able to retire, this rises to 14 per cent of those with four children.

£££   Parents earning £26k–£35k have had their retirement plans impacted the most significantly.

Parents in Wales stopping/reducing retirement saving – 94%

Parents in East Anglia and Midlands stopping/reducing retirement saving – 54%

94 per cent of parents in Wales have had to reduce or stop the amount they save for retirement or put saving for retirement on hold altogether because of the cost of supporting their adult children, compared to 54 per cent in East Anglia and West Midlands.

Source: The Children's Mutual, 'Middle Age Parent Trap' (press release, 16 March 2010). Figures are from their January 2010 Cost of Children research. www.thechildrensmutual.co.uk

show that there is a danger of a huge wealth gap opening up between generations. In his fascinating new book, *The Pinch: How the Baby Boomers Took Their Children's Future – and Why They Should Give It Back*, Willetts argues that the post-war generation benefited from a series of advantageous economic conditions such as free university education, job security and final salary pensions, not to mention rising house prices and high inflation that whittled away mortgage debts. Their children, by contrast, graduate many thousands of pounds in debt, with devalued qualifications, into an environment where employment opportunities are few.

Willetts estimates half of Britain's personal property is owned by the baby boomers – about £3.5 trillion. The over-65s have £2.3 trillion but the assets of people under 45 amount to a pitiful £900 billion. Willetts goes as far as to compare the situation to parents returning home to find a house trashed by a teenage party, only 'what if it's actually the older generation, the baby boomers, who have been leaving behind a mess for the next generation to sort out?'

> ### Willetts estimates half of Britain's personal property is owned by the baby boomers – about £3.5 trillion. The over-65s have £2.3 trillion but the assets of people under 45 amount to a pitiful £900 billion

Willetts, himself a baby boomer and father of two, recalls receiving the odd email 'saying that the book is an outrageous attack on the baby boomers, that this generation is feckless and that they haven't worked hard the way we had to, but mostly people have said that it strikes a chord.'

At the end of last year Lord Mandelson's Department for Business, Innovation and Skills released a condescending guide for parents of boomerang kids. The leaflet urged mums and dads to force their children to do their own washing and ironing; to not provide them with student-friendly snacks or handouts.

But such a guide presumes that a twentysomething graduate enjoys, nay wants, to live with mum and dad. As Willetts points out 'it is not a situation that either parents or kids want to find themselves in. Young adults have the same aspirations as we did when we were their age – it's just that the normal routes to settling down have been blocked.'

So what's his party going to do about it? Willetts says it is vital that stamp duty is cut for first-time buyers,

that there are more incentives to build new housing, that the pension age is raised, and that businesses are encouraged to take on more apprentices. 'To get an apprenticeship at BT now is at least as difficult as getting a place at Oxbridge,' says Willetts. 'Businesses are put off by the cost and the red tape.'

But there are unexpected benefits. Peter is a publishing executive whose 28-year-old daughter moved home after being made redundant. 'I don't think I was ever that close to her when she was a child but that has all changed,' he says. 'Obviously I would love for her to be financially independent but I like that I serve some sort of purpose in her life – there's none of that empty-nest syndrome – and in a way I feel that, by helping her now, she will return the favour when I am elderly.'

A continued bond between parent and child is touching to see, even if it is just £50 loaned close to pay day. In a fractured society, I wonder: is the Yuckie such a bad thing really?

18 February 2010

Empty nest syndrome is a myth, claim scientists

Parents of children who stay at home are more likely to suffer depression than those whose offspring move out, claim scientists in a study that seems to debunk 'empty nest syndrome'.

Researchers said that far from feeling abandoned and lonely, adults with their children living far away seemed happier and more content than those with sons and daughters still living at home or in the local community.

They said that the parents of children who had fled the nest were often from more educated and affluent backgrounds and were proud of their offspring's achievements.

Adults with 'stay at home kids' on the other hand were associated with failed aspiration and inter family conflicts, it was discovered.

Dr Melanie Abas, a psychiatrist at King's College London and lead researcher, said the team was surprised at the findings. 'A commonly held view is that out-migration of young people has starkly negative consequences for parents living in rural areas as they get older,' she said.

She said each of these factors reduced the risk of depression.

In contrast, having fewer children migrate could be linked to failed aspirations, increasing the risk of family conflict and depression, researchers said.

Many parents in Thailand rely on their offspring for money and children who leave home are more likely to be able to send money to support their family, reducing the risk of the depression, the study found.

Dr Abas said: 'While there are obvious difference between Britain and Thailand there are also similarities. In both countries the families are aspirational for their children and in both countries the children leave villages to move to the cities.

'What is surprising is that when all the children move out, you would think the parents would feel desperate but they seem to be holding up very well.'

1 July 2009

Depression was less common among parents whose children lived further away, compared to parents whose children lived locally

'But our findings challenge the popular belief that family separation causes older parents to feel abandoned and lacking in support.'

The study was carried out in villages in rural Thailand, and questioned more than 1,000 parents aged 60 and over.

It found depression was less common among parents whose children lived further away, compared to parents whose children lived locally.

Depression was highest among parents of poorer families with all their children still living in the local area, the study showed.

Dr Abas suggested parents whose children left home tended to be better educated. They were also more likely to be younger, married and still working.

Chapter 2

WORKING PARENTS

Understanding fathering: masculinity, diversity and change

To what extent is there a 'common model' of fatherhood in a modern multicultural Britain that is changing fast?

This research set out to investigate the parenting beliefs and practices of fathers from 29 'ordinary' two-parent families living in non-affluent neighbourhoods from four ethnic groups: White British, Black African, Black Caribbean and Pakistani. The study explores:

⇨ How fathers, mothers and children living in ordinary British families view what it means to be a father.

⇨ How individual interpretations of fatherhood are influenced by personal history, culture, ethnicity, faith and social circumstance.

⇨ Whether it is possible to identify common ideals about fathering and the behaviours of fathers across ethnic groups.

⇨ To what degree members of the same family share beliefs, attitudes and practices.

⇨ How beliefs and practices vary within and across ethnic groups.

⇨ How fathers might be better supported in their roles as parents.

Key points

⇨ More similarities than differences were found in fathers' behaviours, attitudes and aspirations, and the challenges they face.

Children were less likely to base expectations of parenting on parents' gender, suggesting a continuing trend towards fathers' involvement in a broader range of responsibilities

⇨ On the surface the beliefs and attitudes of fathers, mothers and children suggest that parenting roles are less strictly differentiated than they have been: it has become normal to see fathering as multi-dimensional. However, closer examination revealed some traditional gender stereotypes still persisting in practice.

⇨ Certain roles were still seen as predominantly the father's responsibility, namely financial provider and protector. Economic provision still defined the father's role and conceptions of 'good fathering'. Fathers were also viewed as having a key role in discipline.

⇨ Both within families and across ethnic groups, members generally agreed that fathers have a

JOSEPH ROWNTREE FOUNDATION

particularly important role in leisure and play with their children.

⇨ Children were less likely to base expectations of parenting on parents' gender, suggesting a continuing trend towards fathers' involvement in a broader range of responsibilities.

⇨ The values and attitudes fathers described often differed significantly from their actual behaviour. This was due to a combination of practical circumstances, ideas about gender, gender relations within the family, and individual abilities.

Gender stereotypes of parental roles are still alive and well within the family. However, the role of the father continues in its transformation from a traditional one-dimensional role to one that is more multi-dimensional

⇨ The time fathers spent with their children varied considerably across ethnic groups, mainly due to differences in employment and working hours within the sample.

⇨ Across all groups, the largest amount of fathers' time with their children was spent in leisure and play activities at home.

Background

Parents in Britain today show signs of being in the midst of a 'parenting transformation'. Gender stereotypes of parental roles are still alive and well within the family. However, the role of the father continues in its transformation from a traditional one-dimensional role to one that is more multi-dimensional, to meet the current demands of fathering/parenting and the expectation that a father should be involved in all aspects of childcare and child-rearing activities.

Accompanied by a growing body of research evidence endorsing the benefits of 'good parenting', the issue of parenting has been a key policy focus over much of the last decade. Evidence suggests that children benefit significantly when their fathers are actively involved in their care and upbringing. Fathering – what it is and how it can be supported – has in consequence risen higher on the political agenda for UK policy-makers.

The aim of this research was to gain a better understanding of what being a father means to parents and children in four ethnic communities in England: Pakistani, White British, Black Caribbean and Black African. It explored:

⇨ what fathering involves;

⇨ what values and aspirations are attached to fathering; and

⇨ to what extent, in a modern multicultural England that is changing fast, a 'common model' of fatherhood can be identified that holds within and across families from diverse ethnic groups.

The research was based on fathers', mothers' and children's qualitative reports of values, attitudes and behaviours relating to fathering, together with quantitative analysis of their activity diaries.

Values and attitudes

Across the sample there was evidence that values and attitudes concerning the role of fathers were changing. Fathers were expected to engage in all aspects of raising children, assuming a greater multiplicity of roles than ever before. However, consensus on the exact nature of the role – that is, what they should and should not do – was less evident.

Roles such as financial provider and protector continued to be seen as predominantly the responsibility of the father. In particular, economic provision still tends to define the role of the father and remains linked to conceptions of 'good fathering'. Whereas traditionally this one-dimensional approach might have been sufficient to fulfil the paternal role, fathers today are expected to be more than just financial providers, embracing the more multi-dimensional notion of fathering that has now become the norm.

'I think more's expected of fathers now than 30 years ago, 30 years ago the man's responsibility was to go out to work and come home... but I think gradually it's become that way where from a father having maybe ten per cent of the responsibility, his responsibility has gone up, he's going up like 50 per cent... having to learn to have equal responsibility as the mother for what goes on in children's lives and how much you contribute towards them, I think that's what's changed.' (White British father)

Fathers were viewed as having a unique disciplinary role to play, in particular for boys, and more specifically in Black families, where more authoritarian discipline often takes prominence in child-rearing. In both Pakistani and Black families, the father's ability to engender a greater level of respect in their children was seen as important in ensuring that children grow up to be disciplined and well behaved in society. There was a general consensus across all ethnic groups that fathers were more effective disciplinarians than mothers, and were also important role models for their children, especially their sons.

'Boys don't tend to take what I say, they tend to take what he [father] says more, like he's above me, that's how they view it.' (Black Caribbean mother)

JOSEPH ROWNTREE FOUNDATION

'I do think that to bring up a boy child you do need a man to put him in place... the woman can't put them in place because they're turning young men now and they are bigger than their mum, they're stronger than their mums and they wanna do what they wanna do.' (Black Caribbean father)

Many parents believed that a lack of paternal involvement in disciplining children could lead to detrimental outcomes for children and young people that may become more apparent during adolescence, such as lack of respect, delinquency and criminal behaviour. Mothers and children also considered fathers to be important in their role as protectors of the family. The presence of a father made families feel secure and safe, not just in terms of physical safety, but also financially safe, given their role as breadwinner.

Fathers in full-time employment spent significantly less time engaging directly with their children than those who were unemployed or employed part-time

The values and attitudes held by parents in relation to fathers' roles and responsibilities appeared to be quite fluid over time. This was in response to a range of complex and sometimes competing factors, such as practical life circumstances, ideas about gender (individual and societal), gender relations within the family and individual abilities. For example, despite traditional ideas about gender roles, financial difficulties in a family were reflected in changed attitudes to the father as sole financial provider.

For children and young people, values and attitudes around fathers' roles and responsibilities seemed to be largely consistent with the roles that their fathers actually fulfilled.

Fathers' behaviour

The time fathers spent with children was directly linked to the time they had available. Fathers in full-time employment spent significantly less time engaging directly with their children than those who were unemployed or employed part-time.

Fathers spent considerably less time than mothers in physical care-giving, on average only 15 minutes per day, although this increased to twice this time among Black Caribbean fathers. As might be expected, fathers who worked long or irregular hours were less involved in activities such as housework and cooking. On the other hand, fathers who were employed in higher grade

jobs, or who were unemployed, spent greater amounts of time in domestic responsibilities.

Fathers had a special role to fill in playing with their children. The diary records and interviews with all family members revealed that across all ethnic groups, when fathers were involved, leisure activities with children consumed by far the greatest amount of their time. They spent on average three hours per day on play, both at home and outside the home. The middle years of childhood were clearly a key period when fathers had the greatest direct involvement in such activities with their children.

'Without my dad, I really wouldn't be having that much fun.' (Pakistani young person)

Across all families in the sample, fathers spent on average 5.5 hours per day directly engaged in activities with their children. The White British fathers generally spent more time in this way than any of the other ethnic groups, largely due to the higher rate of unemployment and self-employment in this group which resulted in their greater availability.

What shapes fathering?

Own experiences of being parented

Many fathers described having experienced a fairly traditional style of parenting from their own fathers. Fathers of the previous generation were generally confined to the role of breadwinner and disciplinarian, with relatively low levels of involvement in other domains such as child rearing and domestic activities. On the whole, the fathers in this sample showed more differences than similarities with previous generations in their style of fathering, though the extent varied between individuals and ethnic differences were not apparent. In particular, those fathers who described very low levels of paternal engagement and nurturing in their own childhood tended to be more motivated to increase their involvement with their own children.

Gender relations/constructs

Although on the surface parents across all ethnic groups expressed egalitarian views on gender roles and the division of labour, a more traditional view emerged when parents talked in detail about specific roles and responsibilities. More than half of parents across the sample believed the genders to be inherently different in relation to the task of parenting, such that one might be more naturally suited to certain roles than others (for example, mothers more suited to physical care-giving). At the same time, most parents also thought that parents of either gender could competently fulfil most parenting roles if required. Overall, Pakistani and Black African parents tended to hold more traditional views on gender roles in contrast to their White British or Black Caribbean counterparts.

Tradition, culture and religion

Tradition and culture continued to have a strong influence in shaping fathering behaviours and ideals within Pakistani families, and also in some Black Caribbean and Black African families, particularly when the father had been born outside the UK. Parenting practices and ideals across a number of domains such as discipline, financial provision, guiding and monitoring relationships, and encouraging children to learn about parents' culture and religion seemed to be shaped by tradition and culture. At the same time, the findings suggest that the influence of tradition and culture was moderated somewhat by practical, social and cultural factors associated with living in a modern English society.

Current life and family circumstances

Work was the dominant theme with regard to greater paternal involvement: it was both the key constraining factor for those who were employed, and viewed as an enabling factor by those who were unemployed. Long and unsocial hours were frequently cited as being incompatible with family life. Fathers often reported that it was impossible to satisfy the expectation of being a provider as well as having greater involvement in the home. On the other hand, fathers who were unemployed cited their inability to work, and the resulting lack of money, as an equally constraining factor. More family-friendly work patterns with flexible hours and better pay were all identified as facilitating increased levels of paternal involvement.

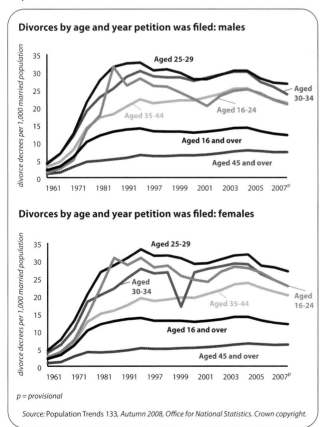

p = provisional

Source: Population Trends 133, Autumn 2008, Office for National Statistics. Crown copyright.

Implications for policy and practice

All of the fathers in the sample, irrespective of ethnic group, were facing similar challenges in their role as parents, largely as a result of practical circumstances such as work commitments, long working hours, unemployment, or poor health. The findings of the study endorse existing and ongoing policy recommendations around supporting and promoting a better work-life balance for fathers, increased financial support for families on low incomes and increased parenting support for fathers.

The similarities in values and attitudes to fathering across the sample, together with fathers' experiences of fatherhood, suggest that support for men in their fathering role and attempts to recruit them into parenting activities might be more successful if they were based upon the shared experiences and commonalities of fathering.

These findings suggest that fathers engage most actively with their children in play and leisure activities during middle childhood. With this in mind, universal services might attract more fathers to participate by designing play and leisure activities appropriate for fathers of primary school-aged children, offered at times – such as evenings and weekends – which are convenient for fathers.

About the project

The findings of this exploratory qualitative study came from a sample comprising 29 'ordinary' two-parent families (father, mother and index child – 87 individuals in total), drawn from areas of England with high rankings on the Index of Multiple Deprivation. Ten Pakistani families were recruited in a metropolitan borough in the North of England, ten White British families were recruited from inner London and cities in the Midlands and North West, and seven Black Caribbean and two Black African families were recruited from the Greater London area. The age range of index children involved in this study was seven to 18 years. Qualitative interviews were conducted with individual family members in their homes, and participants were asked to keep detailed time-use diaries for eight days, to record their daily activities and interactions.

The research was by Hanan Hauari and Katie Hollingworth, Thomas Coram Research Unit
18 September 2009

⇨ The above information is reprinted with kind permission from the Joseph Rowntree Foundation. Please visit this page of their website to view this information: www.jrf.org.uk/publications/understanding-fathering

JOSEPH ROWNTREE FOUNDATION

Fathers struggling to balance work and family

Working dads want more time with their children.

Many British fathers are working long hours, struggling to balance work and family and fear that requesting flexible working will damage their careers, a new report from the Equality and Human Rights Commission has found.

The report, launched today (20 Oct) to coincide with Parents' Week, finds that British men want to take a more active role in caring for their children. But four in ten fathers say they spend too little time with their children.

45 per cent of men fail to take two weeks' paternity leave after the birth of their child with the most common reason provided being because they can't afford to. Two in five men fear that asking for flexible working arrangements would result in their commitment to their job being questioned and would negatively affect their chances of a promotion.

The report also points to an opportunity for employers to gain a competitive advantage in recruitment, as two in three fathers consider the availability of flexible working to be important when looking for a new job.

One approach to balancing work and family commitments outlined in the report is to expand paternity and parental leave schemes. The Commission has previously outlined a series of fully costed policies that would help to meet the needs of businesses and modern families as part of its Working Better initiative.

It included fathers having:

⇨ two weeks' paternity leave at the birth of their child at 90 per cent pay

⇨ four months of dedicated 'parental leave' with at least eight weeks of leave being at 90 per cent pay

⇨ another four months' parental leave – that can be taken by either mother or father – eight weeks of which is taken at 90 per cent pay.

Andrea Murray, Acting Group Director Strategy from the Equality and Human Rights Commission said:

'It is clear that today's families require a modern approach to balancing work and childcare commitments. Fathers are telling us they are not spending enough time with their families and want to take a more active role in shaping the lives of their children.

'We have spoken to parents, employers, unions and leading academic experts in the field, and we believe that our Working Better policies lay out a road-map to 2020 which will put Britain ahead of the curve in terms of modern working practices.

Six in ten fathers said they worked more than 40 hours a week

'Two-thirds of fathers see flexible working as an important benefit when looking for a new job. This highlights an opportunity for British businesses to use flexible working as an incentive for attracting and retaining the most talented of employees. Some companies which have adopted forward thinking policies towards families are reporting increased productivity, reduction in staff turnover, reduced training costs and an ability to respond better to customer requirements.'

Notes

Current and proposed Government paternity leave arrangements include:

⇨ Two weeks' statutory paternity leave paid at a flat rate of up to £123.06 per week.

⇨ A proposal that by 2011 fathers will be able to take another six months' paternity – three months at the statutory rate of pay and three months' unpaid – as long as the mother gives up six months of maternity leave.

Other key statistics:

⇨ Six in ten fathers said they worked more than 40 hours a week.

⇨ Half of fathers believed they spent too much time at work.

⇨ Nearly six in ten fathers agreed with the statement that partners can share work/career and childcare equally.

⇨ Although flexible working was available to half of fathers, only 30 per cent were actually using it.

EQUALITY AND HUMAN RIGHTS COMMISSION

⇨ 56 per cent of fathers who took paternity leave said that taking time off around the birth of their child led to them taking a greater role in caring for their children, while 69 per cent said it led to improvements in family life.

⇨ Of those who did not take paternity leave, two thirds said they would have liked to 'a lot'. The most common reason provided for not doing so was being unable to afford to take the time off.

⇨ 61 per cent of fathers supported the idea of an additional four weeks paid leave that would be reserved solely for the father, with 55 per cent saying they would take this kind of leave if it was available.

20 October 2009

⇨ The copyright and all other intellectual property rights in *Fathers struggling to balance work and family* are owned by, or licensed to, the Commission for Equality and Human Rights, known as the Equality and Human Rights Commission ("the EHRC"). Visit www.ehrc.gov.uk for more information.

Stay-at-home mothers 'suffer more stress than City traders'

Caring for young children at home is one of the most stressful occupations, a study says.

By Claire Smith

Researchers compared the levels of the stress hormone cortisol in people working as taxi drivers, teachers, nurses, City traders and stay-at-home parents. Those who were dealing with young children at home were found to have higher levels than any other group.

'Stay-at-home parents receive little or no training and are typically isolated from other adults for much of the day'

Dr David Lewis, of the Mindlab Organisation, which carried out the research, said: 'The key here is the degree of control each of these professionals feel able to exercise over their lives. The greater their personal sense of control, the better they deal with the stress.

'Stay-at-home parents receive little or no training and are typically isolated from other adults for much of the day.'

He added: 'The key to managing stay-at-home stress is to develop strategies that enable them to prevent small stresses from developing into bigger ones. This can often be done quickly by taking some selfish time out on a daily basis.'

Professor Cary Cooper, head of psychology and health at Lancaster University and an expert on stress, said he was not surprised to hear childcare was rated as most stressful.

'I think it is one of the most difficult jobs in the world. It's like herding cats. Young children are very active and they have no concept of what is safe.

'Other jobs are a doddle in comparison. Most stay-at-home parents are women and a lot have the added stress of feeling guilty because they think society expects them to be working. Things are more difficult than 20 or 30 years ago when women lived nearer to extended families and had a support network.'

Professor Cooper said too much stress could cause health problems, and the key was to have time away from the children.

Tom Roberts, head of public affairs for Children 1st, said: 'These findings are not a surprise to us. A recent report based on calls to our ParentLine Scotland service showed that parents did feel a lot of pressure.

'It was often external pressures that caused the most concern. This included feeling pressure to be the perfect parent, alongside personal issues such as loneliness and isolation.

'We also know that callers are often keen to access support but can't always find that support available locally. This makes things especially difficult for those who don't have family and friends able to help out.'

Jenni Trent Hughes, a US psychologist and broadcaster specialising in family issues, said: 'The answer is simply to be selfish and take some time out.

'If you're not taking care of yourself then how can you properly take care of anyone else? If you're short-tempered, tired or at your wits' end how can you be the best you can be for your partner, children, family and – last but not least – yourself?'

First published in The Scotsman, *12 September 2009*

EQUALITY AND HUMAN RIGHTS COMMISSION / THE SCOTSMAN

Work and family

Two-thirds of mums are in employment.

More than two thirds of working-age women with dependent children (68 per cent) were in employment in the second quarter of 2008. But women without children were more likely to be in employment, at 73 per cent over the same period.

The age of the youngest child affects the employment rate of mothers. Of working-age women with children aged under five, 57 per cent were in employment. This compared with 71 per cent for those whose youngest child was aged five to ten and 78 per cent whose youngest child was aged 11 to 15.

Conversely, men with dependent children are more likely than those without to be in employment. The age of their children has no impact on their likelihood of being in employment. Around 90 per cent of men with dependent children were in employment regardless of the age of their youngest child.

Women are more likely than men to work part time, particularly if they have dependent children. 38 per cent of women with dependent children worked part time compared with 22 per cent of those without dependent children. Only four per cent of men with dependent children and seven per cent of men without dependent children worked part time.

A smaller proportion of lone mothers are in employment than mothers who are married or cohabiting. Fifty six per cent of lone mothers were in employment, compared with 72 per cent of married or cohabiting women with dependent children.

The age of the youngest dependent child has an impact on the employment rate of lone mothers. 35 per cent of those with a child aged under five were in employment compared with 59 per cent of those with a child aged five to ten. The difference in employment rates between lone mothers and married or cohabiting women narrowed as the age of the youngest child rose, almost disappearing for women with dependent children aged 16 to 18.

The opportunity to work flexibly can improve people's ability to balance home and work responsibilities. In Q22008 women were more likely than men to have some form of flexible working arrangement, including flexible working hours and term-time working arrangements. Around 30 per cent of women used a flexible working pattern as compared to around 20 per cent of men. Flexible working arrangements among men and women with dependent children show a similar story. Just under a third of mothers used some form of flexible working pattern compared with around a fifth of fathers.

Among all types of flexible working arrangements, flexible working hours was the most common type to be used by all parent employees (ten per cent). Of parents with dependent children, mothers were slightly more likely to use this working arrangement than fathers; one in nine mothers worked flexible working hours compared with one in 11 fathers. Term-time working arrangements, however, showed the largest difference between mothers and fathers – nine per cent of mothers used this type of flexible working arrangement compared with one per cent of fathers.

Source: Labour Force Survey, Q2 2008, Office for National Statistics

Notes:

⇨ Employment rate – the proportion of the population of working-age men (aged 16–64) and women (aged 16–59) who are in employment.

⇨ Dependent children – children aged under 16 and those aged 16 to 18 who are never-married and in full-time education.

⇨ Data are at Q2 2008 and are not seasonally adjusted.

26 September 2008

⇨ The above information is reprinted with kind permission from the Office for National Statistics. Visit www.statistics.gov.uk for more information.

© *Crown copyright*

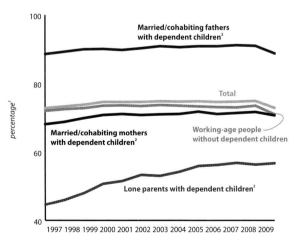

Employment rates of working age people[1] by parental status (figures for April-June of each year).

Married/cohabiting fathers with dependent children[2]

Total

percentage[3]

Married/cohabiting mothers with dependent children[2]

Working-age people without dependent children

Lone parents with dependent children[2]

1997 1998 1999 2000 2001 2002 2003 2004 2005 2006 2007 2008 2009

1. Men aged 16-64 and women aged 16-59.
2. Children under 16 and those aged 16-18 who are never married and in full-time education.
3. Base for percentages excludes people with unknown employment status.

Source: ONS Labour Force Survey. Crown copyright.

A guide to maternity rights

Information from NetDoctor.

Written by Rebecca Sheasby, journalist

Most women have the right to take up to 52 weeks' maternity leave (ML). During this time, you'll get Statutory Maternity Pay (SMP) or Maternity Allowance (MA) for up to 39 weeks, depending on your situation.

To make sure you're fully in the picture about your maternity rights, we've put together this guide to statutory maternity rights – the minimum you're entitled to by law.

Don't forget, some employers offer better benefits than these, so check your contract first.

Basic rights

New basic rights

New rules that extend SMP, MA and Statutory Adoption Pay (SAP) from 39 weeks to 52 weeks are likely to be introduced at the end of 2009.

On top of this, the Government is introducing Additional Paternity Leave and Pay [APL&P].

This will give employed fathers the right to take up to an additional 26 weeks off work, with pay, to care for their child in its first year if the mother has returned to work and had not used her full entitlement to paid maternity leave.

No matter how long you've worked for a company or whether you work part time, every pregnant employee is entitled to some basic rights.

⇨ Paid time off for antenatal leave. This can include relaxation and parentcraft classes.

⇨ Suspension from work on full pay if there is an unavoidable health and safety risk and an alternative job cannot be found.

⇨ 26 weeks' ordinary maternity leave (OML) during which all the normal terms and conditions of your contract apply, apart from salary.

⇨ The right not to suffer unfair treatment, be dismissed or selected for redundancy on grounds related to your pregnancy or maternity leave.

⇨ Free dental care and NHS prescriptions for the length of your pregnancy and up to 12 months after the birth.

⇨ The right to return to work after maternity leave ends.

Protecting your pregnant health

Once an employer receives written notification of your pregnancy, they must carry out a health and safety risk assessment. You are entitled to see a copy of the report.

As well as hazards such as exposure to certain chemicals, risks include lifting heavy loads, standing for long periods and jobs which involve a lot of travel.

If the risk can't be avoided, your employer must offer you a suitable alternative job or suspend you from work on full pay for the duration of your pregnancy.

If you work nights and have a medical certificate that states it could affect the health of you or baby, your employer must offer you suitable daytime work or suspend you on full pay.

If a pregnancy-related illness causes you to be absent from work in the last four weeks of pregnancy, maternity leave will start automatically. Before then, time off would be taken as sick leave.

Ordinary maternity leave (OML)

All pregnant employees are entitled to 26 weeks' ordinary maternity leave. All terms and conditions of your contract, apart from salary, apply during this time – including perks such as health club membership or use of a mobile phone.

What if my baby is born early?

Maternity leave will begin automatically on the day after the birth, regardless of your intended start date.

SMP will start the day after your first day off work.

To preserve your rights, let your employer know as soon as possible the date of your baby's birth.

The earliest you can start ordinary maternity leave is 11 weeks before the expected week of childbirth – about week 29 of pregnancy.

To take OML, you must notify your employer of your intentions by the 15th week before your expected week of childbirth – i.e. before you are 26 weeks pregnant. You will need to let your employer know the expected week of childbirth and the date you intend to start leave.

If your employer requests confirmation of your pregnancy, you will need to provide a medical certificate (MAT B1) signed by a GP or midwife that states the expected week of childbirth.

Once your employer has received this notification, they must confirm the date you are due to return. After you receive this, you don't have to give your employer any

further notification as your maternity leave comes to an end, unless you want to change the date you return.

If you want to change when you start or return from ordinary maternity leave, you will need to give your employer 28 days' notice.

Returning to work after OML

You are entitled to return to the same job on the same terms as before leave started. You are also entitled to benefit from any other improvements in terms of pay, holiday, etc. that have been introduced.

Pay

During ordinary maternity leave, most pregnant employees are entitled to either statutory maternity pay or maternity allowance. The amount you're entitled to depends on how much you earn and how long you've worked for your current employer.

Statutory maternity pay (SMP)

⇨ SMP is paid by your employer for up to 39 weeks, depending on whether you decide to return early from maternity leave.

⇨ It is paid in the same way as your salary would normally be, i.e. weekly or monthly.

⇨ For the first six weeks your employer pays 90 per cent of your average earnings.

⇨ For the remaining 33 weeks, you will receive the standard rate of £123.06 per week.

⇨ If you earn less than £123.06 per week, you will receive 90 per cent of your average earnings for the 33 weeks.

Do you qualify for SMP?

To qualify for SMP:

⇨ you must have worked for your employer for 26 weeks by the 15th week before the expected week of childbirth;

⇨ you must earn at least £84 a week;

⇨ you must give your employer at least four weeks' notice of the date you intend to start maternity leave.

It is up to your employer to decide whether you qualify for SMP. If you don't, your employer must give you form SMP1 stating why you don't qualify.

Reasons why you may not qualify SMP

⇨ You work on a freelance basis (i.e. are self-employed).

⇨ You haven't worked at the company for long enough.

⇨ You don't earn the minimum £84 per week.

⇨ You haven't given 28 days' notice of when you intend to start maternity leave.

⇨ You haven't given medical evidence of your pregnancy within the time allowed – your company cannot pay SMP until it receives maternity certificate MAT B1.

If you disagree with your employer's decision, you can ask for a formal decision from the Inland Revenue.

If you don't qualify for SMP, you may be entitled to maternity allowance, which you need to claim from your local social security/Jobcentre Plus office.

After the birth

After you have worked for a company for one year, you will be entitled to 13 weeks' unpaid parental leave to be taken before your child's fifth birthday. This leave is on top of your usual holiday entitlement.

Coping with the unexpected

In addition to parental leave, you have the right to take time off work to deal with family emergencies, no matter how long you've worked for a company.

Parents of disabled children are entitled to 18 weeks' unpaid leave to be taken before their child's 18th birthday.

You are entitled to this leave for each child under five born after 15 December 1999 (or under 18 for disabled children).

Parental leave is time off to look after your child or make arrangements for their welfare. You can use it simply to spend more time with your children while they are young.

How to claim

The terms that apply to taking parental leave can be agreed on an individual basis between yourself and your employer. If there is no agreement in place, the 'fallback scheme' comes into force.

The fallback scheme

⇨ Leave must be taken in blocks of one week. Parents of disabled children may take leave in multiples of one day.

⇨ You can only take four weeks' parental leave each year per child.

⇨ You must give your employer 21 days' notice.

⇨ Your employer can postpone leave for up to six months if it would disrupt business.

⇨ The above information is reprinted with kind permission from NetDoctor. Visit www.netdoctor.co.uk for more.

© NetDoctor

NETDOCTOR

Dads at work: your rights

More than half of fathers want flexible working arrangements when they look for work, a new survey has shown. But many fathers are unaware of their rights to paternity leave and flexible work arrangements. A new campaign, 'Dads at Work', launches today to make dads more aware of these workplace rights.

Flexibility is important to fathers

Flexible working is a big factor for modern dads who want to take care of their children, according to figures published today by the Department for Business, Innovation and Skills (BIS).

More than half (56 per cent) of dads with children aged 16 and under said they look for employers that offer flexible working when choosing a new job.

> ### One in five fathers with children aged 16 or under was unaware that, by law, they can request flexible working

Nearly two thirds (62 per cent) believe their relationship with their child will suffer if they're not at home after the baby is born.

Paternity leave and flexible working – rights for dads

Fathers are entitled to:

⇨ paternity leave – new dads can take two weeks' leave paid at a standard rate, if they notify their employer 15 weeks before the due date

⇨ parental leave – dads also have the right to take up to 13 weeks' unpaid leave until their child is five years old.

Nearly all dads with children aged five or under (91 per cent) think it's important that they have the option to take paid paternity leave. But one in three parents with children under five did not realise that paid paternity leave is law, the survey found. The two-week paternity leave is paid at a standard rate (currently £123.06 per week).

One in five fathers surveyed also did not know that to access full paternity rights, they need to speak with their employer 15 weeks before their baby is due.

Flexible working rights

Parents of a child aged 16 or under are also entitled to request flexible working – such as flexi-time, part-time or working from home. By law, their employer must seriously consider the request.

One in five fathers with children aged 16 or under was unaware that, by law, they can request flexible working. Over 90 per cent of such requests are approved by employers.

Awareness campaign for dads

As the campaign to inform fathers of their rights was launched, Employment Relations Minister Lord Young said it was 'all about making sure dads know what they can do and helping them weigh up what works best for them and their family. The key is to talk to their employer.'

WOULD YOU MIND WALKING HER, WHILE I FINISH YOUR PROJECT CHIEF?

The month-long campaign will see posters and leaflets distributed at doctors' surgeries, hospitals and antenatal clinics. These direct fathers to the Dads at work website.

Online advertising will also appear on websites that attract high volumes of 'dad' visitors.

18 February 2010

⇨ The above information is reprinted with kind permission from Directgov. Visit www.direct.gov.uk for more information.

DIRECTGOV

⇨ In 2006, 23 per cent of children in Great Britain were living in lone-parent families. This has increased from 21 per cent in 1997 and seven per cent in 1972. (page 1)

⇨ Married couples could make up 41 per cent of the over-16 population in 20 years' time. The figure is 49 per cent now. Single people, divorcees, lone parents and cohabiting couples will outnumber them. (page 3)

⇨ While 'tough love' parenting is less frequent in low-income backgrounds, the 'love' element was consistently distributed throughout economic groups. Consistent rule-setting and authoritative parenting was associated with wealthier families, indicating a need for parents to set more consistent discipline and boundaries in lower-income groups. (page 6)

⇨ Half of couples divorcing in 2008 had at least one child aged under 16. There were 106,763 children aged under 16 who were in families where the parents divorced in 2008, a decrease of 29 per cent from 1998 when there were 150,129 children. Over one-fifth (21 per cent) of the children in 2008 were under five and 63 per cent were under 11. (page 8)

⇨ Children's positive adjustment to family breakdown is associated with a number of factors. These include competent and warm parenting, parents having good mental health, low parental conflict, cooperative parenting post separation, and social support. (page 9)

⇨ Stepfamilies are the fastest growing family type in the UK. Over one-third of us are part of the stepfamily experience. (page 10)

⇨ One in three children whose parents separated or divorced over the last 20 years disclosed that they had lost contact permanently with their father. (page 11)

⇨ Half of single parents are poor and their children are twice as likely to be poor as those in couple families. (page 13)

⇨ The proportion of single grandparents doubled between 1998 and 2007. This does not include widows. 36% of single grandmothers are aged under 55. (page 14)

⇨ The value of the grandparental childcare contribution has been calculated at £3.9 billion. One in three families depend on grandparents for childcare. (page 17)

⇨ Nearly everyone who completes the adoption process – 94% – is recommended to adopt. (page 18)

⇨ One in four people in the UK have an adoption connection – adoption is part of the fabric of modern family life. (page 19)

⇨ 57% of children adopted in 2008 were aged between one and four. 24% were aged between five and nine. (page 21)

⇨ Between 2007 and 2009 the number of gay men approved to adopt doubled. (page 22)

⇨ Figures published in the annual ONS 'state of the nation' report *Social Trends* show that, in the second quarter of 2008, 29 per cent of 20- to 34-year-old men and 18 per cent of women of the same age lived with their parents. This equated to around 1.8 million men and 1.1 million women. (page 26)

⇨ 57% of parents of 18- to 30-year-olds say they have no choice but to retire later, with four in ten (43%) expecting to work up to five years longer than they wanted because of the cost of their 'adult' children. (page 27)

⇨ Parents of children who stay at home are more likely to suffer depression than those whose offspring move out, claim scientists in a study that seems to debunk 'empty nest syndrome'. (page 29)

⇨ Parents in Britain today show signs of being in the midst of a 'parenting transformation'. Gender stereotypes of parental roles are still alive and well within the family. However, the role of the father continues in its transformation from a traditional one-dimensional role to one that is more multi-dimensional. (page 31)

⇨ Many British fathers are working long hours, struggling to balance work and family and fear that requesting flexible working will damage their careers, a new report from the Equality and Human Rights Commission has found. (page 34)

⇨ Researchers compared the levels of the stress hormone cortisol in people working as taxi drivers, teachers, nurses, City traders and stay-at-home parents. Those who were dealing with young children at home were found to have higher levels than any other group. (page 35)

Adoption

When a child is adopted, an individual or couple apply to become the child's parents. Once the court order is granted, the adopters become the child's legal guardians in the way that their birth parents previously were, and the biological parents cease to have any legal rights over the child.

This is different from fostering, where families will provide a stable home for children on a temporary basis. Although some children do stay with their foster family long-term, fosterers do not become the child's legal parents.

Authoritarian-strict parenting

This type of parenting places a strong emphasis on control and clear limits above warmth and involvement.

Baby boomers

Name given to the generation born during the period of increased birth rates following the second world war, i.e. in the late 1940s and 1950s.

Balanced-authoritative parenting

A parenting style which balances clear limits and appropriate expectations with warmth and involvement.

Cohabiting couple

Two people who live together as a couple but are not married or in a civil partnership. Current trends suggest more couples are choosing to have children in cohabiting rather than married relationships.

Dependent children

Usually defined as persons aged under 16, or 16 to 18 and in full-time education, who are part of a family unit and living in the household.

Empty nest syndrome

Feelings of sadness and depression experienced when one or more children leave home. More commonly associated with mothers, these feelings can occur in either or both parents.

Family

A domestic group related by blood, marriage or other familial ties living together in a household. A 'traditional' or nuclear family usually refers to one in which a married heterosexual couple raise their biological children together; however, changing family structures has resulted in so-called 'non-traditional' family groups including stepfamilies, families with adopted or foster children, single-parent families and children being raised by same-sex parents.

Hands-off parenting

Parents following this style tend to be laissez-faire, less involved and with fewer boundaries.

Lone/single parent

Someone who is raising a child alone, either due to divorce/separation, widowhood, an absent parent or due to single adoption. The majority of lone parents are women.

Parental responsibility

When an adult has the legal right to take responsibility for the care and well-being of their child(ren) and can make important decisions about things such as food, clothing and education, this is referred to as parental responsibility. Married couples having children together automatically have this right, as do all mothers, but if the parents are unmarried the father only has parental responsibility if certain conditions are met.

Permissive-indulgent parenting

A parenting style where the parents are warm and engaged with their children but with fewer or inconsistent limits and expectations compared with balanced-authoritative parents.

Stepfamily

Stepfamilies come together when people marry again or live with a new partner. This may be after the death of one parent, separation or divorce. It can also mean that children from different families end up living together for all or part of the time. One in four children has parents who get divorced and over half of their mothers and fathers will remarry or repartner to form a stepfamily.

Additional Resources

Other Issues titles

If you are interested in researching further some of the issues raised in *The Changing Family,* you may like to read the following titles in the *Issues* series:

⇨ Vol. 183 *Work and Employment* (ISBN 978 1 86168 524 7)

⇨ Vol. 182 *Teenage Conceptions* (ISBN 978 1 86168 523 0)

⇨ Vol. 178 *Reproductive Ethics* (ISBN 978 1 86168 502 5)

⇨ Vol. 166 *Marriage and Cohabitation* (ISBN 978 1 86168 470 7)

⇨ Vol. 160 *Poverty and Exclusion* (ISBN 978 1 86168 453 0)

⇨ Vol. 159 *An Ageing Population* (ISBN 978 1 86168 452 3)

⇨ Vol. 155 *Domestic Abuse* (ISBN 978 1 86168 442 4)

⇨ Vol. 154 *The Gender Gap* (ISBN 978 1 86168 441 7)

⇨ Vol. 153 *Sexual Orientation and Society* (ISBN 978 1 86168 440 0)

For a complete list of available *Issues* titles, please visit our website: www.independence.co.uk/shop

Useful organisations

You may find the websites of the following organisations useful for further research:

⇨ **After Adoption:** www.afteradoption.org.uk

⇨ **BAAF:** www.baaf.org.uk

⇨ **Centre for Research on Families and Relationships:** www.crfr.ac.uk

⇨ **The Children's Mutual:** www.thechildrensmutual.co.uk

⇨ **Demos:** www.demos.co.uk

⇨ **Department for Communities and Local Government:** www.dclg.gov.uk

⇨ **Equality and Human Rights Commission:** www.ehrc.gov.uk

⇨ **Family Matters Institute:** www.familymatters.org.uk

⇨ **Families Online:** www.familiesonline.co.uk

⇨ **Family and Parenting Institute:** www.familyandparenting.org

⇨ **Gingerbread:** www.gingerbread.org.uk

⇨ **Grandparents Plus:** www.grandparentsplus.org.uk

⇨ **Joseph Rowntree Foundation:** www.jrf.org.uk

For more book information, visit our website...

www.independence.co.uk

Information available online includes:

✓ Detailed descriptions of titles

✓ Tables of contents

✓ Facts and figures

✓ Online ordering facilities

✓ Log-in page for Issues Online (an Internet resource available free to Firm Order Issues subscribers – ask your librarian to find out if this service is available to you)

ACKNOWLEDGEMENTS

The publisher is grateful for permission to reproduce the following material.

While every care has been taken to trace and acknowledge copyright, the publisher tenders its apology for any accidental infringement or where copyright has proved untraceable. The publisher would be pleased to come to a suitable arrangement in any such case with the rightful owner.

Chapter One: About Depression

Marriage, relationships and family trends, © Family and Parenting Institute, Couples, and children of couples, by year of divorce [graph], © Crown copyright is reproduced with the permission of Her Majesty's Stationery Office, Data shows continuing changes to marriage and society in the UK, © Ekklesia, What's your parenting style?, © Dr Clare Bailey, 'Character' is the key to social mobility, © Demos, Divorces in England and Wales, © Crown copyright is reproduced with the permission of Her Majesty's Stationery Office, Impact of family breakdown on children's wellbeing, © Crown copyright is reproduced with the permission of Her Majesty's Stationery Office, A new family, © Care for the Family, Broken families and paternal contact, © Telegraph Media Group Limited 2009, Lone-parent families with young children, © Centre for Research on Families and Relationships, Single parents bear the brunt of the slump, © Gingerbread, Do grandparents matter?, © Family Matters, Grandparents and poverty [graphs], © Grandparents Plus, Grandparents not always the most effective childcarers, © Institute of Education, University of London, Grandparents and childcare [graphs], © Grandparents Plus, Thinking of adopting, © After Adoption, Key facts about adoption, © After Adoption, The best thing we've ever done, © BAAF, Adoptions by date of court order [graph], © Crown copyright is reproduced with the permission of Her Majesty's Stationery Office, The rise of the gay dad, © Guardian News and Media Limited 2009, Adoption order by date of court order and whether child born within/outside marriage [graph], © Crown copyright is reproduced with the permission of Her Majesty's Stationery Office, Nearly a third of young men live with their parents, © Crown copyright is reproduced with the permission of Her Majesty's Stationery Office, Today's young adults can't afford to let go, © Telegraph Media Group Limited 2010, Research from the Children's Mutual [graph], © The Children's Mutual, Empty nest syndrome is a myth, claim scientists, © Telegraph Media Group Limited 2010.

Chapter Two: Working Parents

Understanding fathering: masculinity, diversity and change, © Joseph Rowntree Foundation, Divorces by age and year petition was filed [graph], © Crown copyright is reproduced with the permission of Her Majesty's Stationery Office, Fathers struggling to balance work and family, © Equality and Human Rights Commission, Stay-at-home mothers 'suffer more stress than City traders', © Claire Smith, Work and family, © Crown copyright is reproduced with the permission of Her Majesty's Stationery Office, Employment rates of working-age people by parental status [graph], © Crown copyright is reproduced with the permission of Her Majesty's Stationery Office, A guide to maternity rights, © NetDoctor, Dads at work: your rights, © Crown copyright is reproduced with the permission of Her Majesty's Stationery Office.

Illustrations

Pages 1, 9, 23, 28, 39: Don Hatcher; pages 3, 15, 26, 30: Angelo Madrid; pages 7, 12, 20, 29: Simon Kneebone; pages 8, 16: Bev Aisbett.

Cover photography

Left: © Roland Seeger. Centre: © Randa Clay. Right: © Scott Liddell.

Additional acknowledgements

Research by Robert Fletcher.

Additional research by Hart McLeod Limited, Cambridge.

With thanks to the Independence team: Mary Chapman, Sandra Dennis and Jan Sunderland.

Lisa Firth
Cambridge
May, 2010